# Pearl Hunters

*Becoming a people of presence*

Stewart Keiller

Blessings

Stewart Keiller

**INTEGRITY**
MEDIA EUROPE

Integrity Media Europe
Unit 1 Hargreaves Business Park
Hargreaves Road
Eastbourne
BN23 6QW

www.worshipwithintegrity.com
www.iworship24-7.com

ISBN 978-1-907080-10-4

Printed in Malta

# What others are saying about
## *Pearl Hunters*

"There is no greater priority in our lives than the pursuit of the presence of God. Stewart's book is an honest and heartfelt rallying cry for today's churches to put first things first and to go hunting for the pearl of the Father's presence. I pray that it will stir you as deeply as it has stirred me."

Dr Mark Stibbe
www.fathershousetrust.com

"Stewart Keiller has a passion for the release of the supernatural power of God's Kingdom, not only in his community but the world at large. That kind of power only comes from an ever-deepening relationship with the Lord, so Stewart has written a book that prods into the hearts of all God's people, stirring them up to seek similar encounters in their lives and communities, no matter what it takes. It is this kind of passion, this consuming fire, that God is seeking in His people, and I am convinced He is faithful to reward them with a greater expression of His love and power. Stewart's book is a catalyst for this expression and it requires us all to pay attention to what he has to say!"

Dr. James Maloney
President, The ACTS Group International
Author of *The Dancing Hand of God*

"It would be trite to label *Pearl Hunters* as a 'gem', but the fact is, it truly is reflective of the Pearl of Great Price, Jesus. True to Stewart's personality and ministry this book is thoughtful, loaded with wisdom and provocative. What sets *Pearl Hunters* apart from the plethora of books focused on the need to know God experientially is that Stewart gives us a balanced, biblical perspective on not only treasuring what God values, but the guidelines He gives us for pursuing His Presence and living in it. His biblically based encouragement and insights on the mixture of faith, love, fear, and grace-based obedience are both practical and doable! I highly recommend that you get your own copy and dive into it!"

Marc A. Dupont
Mantle of Praise Ministries, Inc.

"Stewart Keiller, in his playful and outspoken style, will grip you with the all important question: Will you pursue and find that which is to die for? It is the only thing worth living for! I couldn't put this book down."

John Arnott
Cath the Fire Ministries and
Partners in Harvest

# Contents

Dedication 6

Preface 7

Foreword by Steve Witt 9

Chapter 1    Distinctive 11

Chapter 2    "Go With Us" 25

Chapter 3    Experiencing Encounter 39

Chapter 4    Obey 53

Chapter 5    Promises 65

Chapter 6    Fear, Frustration and Fatigue 81

Chapter 7    Glory 95

Chapter 8    Holy, Holy, Holy 111

Chapter 9    People of Presence 127

Chapter 10    Pursuit 143

Chapter 11    Deeper 159

Chapter 12    Pearly Gates 175

# Dedication

To Deborah – wife, friend, mother, artist, wild goose!

To Paul and Vicky – the greatest pearl hunters I know.

# Preface

It is said we should "Keep the main thing the main thing". Useful advice. I wonder then, why we don't apply it to our spiritual lives? We fill our lives with just about everything else except God! Moses really got it right: "I'm not going any further unless you go with us God." There is no point in being the people of God unless we have God with us! At one point I was going to call this book, "Without God We Are Stuffed" – it's so true.

I approach this book on the presence of God from the point of view of someone who has realised you can have a fancy programme, a great building, a huge, affluent church making a real difference in its city, but if you don't have God in the centre guiding you by His Spirit then you really don't have anything at all. I think many of us have tasted the power and reality of God, but then sold out to something more alluring. We seem to have a knack of getting disillusioned and then allowing our emotions or thoughts to take centre stage, rather than submitting ourselves to the power of God.

I have been surrounded by some great "presence people" in my life – people who have made a passionate lifestyle of pursuing God at all costs. This book is for them and for those who aspire to a life of pursuing His presence. I hope these words and thoughts reflect something of the price such people have had to pay, even if sometimes they feel they have gone up a few cul-de-sacs. I pray that this book will inspire and provoke others to join in the hunt for the abiding presence of God. It is never too late to join! You are never too old run, never too broken to be fixed, never to dirty to be holy. Never say never!

*Stewart Keiller,*
*June 2010*

# Foreword

I've known Stewart for a number of years and have enjoyed his unique blend of gifting, strategic thinking, and childlike openness to the Holy Spirit. All of this converges in an "anointed frustration" in a man who wants to blaze a trail for passionate thinkers. Where are the new John Wesley's? Where are the next D. L. Moody's? The list could go on, but few contemporaries come to mind.

Stewart's book is meant to be provoking. It is sometimes subtle and self-effacing, and at other times sounds like a coach calling his team to become champions. It raises the valid question, *"Is the Christianity we witness in the Western world on a par with that we read about in Scripture?"* Today, seeking holiness is deemed as being judgmental. Clarity is seen as intolerance. Passion in worship is looked on as extremism. Where are the passionate, radical followers of Christ? Where are the followers of Christ who only care about His opinion and His alone?

The men and women of the book of Acts were recognised as having "been with Jesus". This marked them with boldness. It was a trait that superseded any intimidation of education, culture or class that was levelled against them. It set them apart. Wherever they went they changed the spiritual atmosphere by their very presence. They were the fragrance of hope in a decaying world. They were the purveyors of the great exchange of Heaven: beauty for ashes, joy for mourning, a garment of praise for a spirit of heaviness! They came from God's presence with the anointing that only an encounter with Him can bring. They changed a culture, made a difference, and went to their just reward.

Read this book differently than others. Read a chapter, put it down, and then allow the Holy Spirit to soften and transform your heart. By the end of the book you may step into the line of men and women throughout the ages who boldly declare, *"I fought the good fight, I finished the course, I kept the faith ..."* You will be a part of an emerging generation that cares not for its own soul, but longs for the emergence of the King and His kingdom.

Don't be conformed – be transformed!

*Steve Witt,*
*Author and Senior Leader, Bethel Cleveland*

# Distinctive

*"They all look the same!"*

Let's imagine, for a moment, an angelic conversation. Put aside any theological problems you may have with angels talking for a minute, I'm not trying to make any theological point!

One angel is looking at what's happening on earth on a huge plasma screen (I hope they have them in heaven. Otherwise, what am I going to watch movies on?) He looks forlorn, saddened by the vivid images flashing across the screen. He is almost motionless, deeply engrossed, concentrating on every movement of the humans he is watching. Something is clearly troubling him. Another angel arrives.

"What movie are you watching?"

"Oh, just the saints of God on earth. It is set somewhere in England, a nice town, very peaceful," replies the human-watching angel.

"What's happened so far?" asks the new angel.

"Um, not really sure. It's a bit slow moving. Basically, the saints of God are dispersed through the town, going about their daily business, and every Sunday they get together for a sing song and one of their number shouts at them for half an hour."

"Doesn't seem very interesting! Do you think it's going to get any more exciting than this?" The second angel is now moving towards the door, having seen enough of the human movie.

"I hope so," replies the first. "It's supposed to get very exciting. I've read the Book, so I know what happens at the end of the story. But this bit is so boring!"

Having lost his concentration, the human-watching angel tries to find something to hold his attention, but he is distracted.

"Well, who is who?" asks angel number, about to depart. "I can't tell the Saints apart from anyone else."

"That's the problem," says the watching angel, now standing with the remote in his hand, ready to end the program. "They all look the same!".

And with that he switches channel to a movie about the life of the great John Wesley. "Hey, this is more like it," he calls after his colleague.

## The Church is not distinctive!

We have a problem Church. Please don't mistake me. I am not, of course, referring to you the reader, or speaking about the church you represent, or even the Church in many parts of the Western world. Ok, I might be, but since you have only just begun reading, I don't want to put you off just yet! For now, let me say, "We have a problem western-church-not-including-anyone-reading-this-book":

*We look the same as everyone else!*

We work like everyone else, we shop like everyone else, we drive cars like everyone else (although some drive much nicer cars than others). We get married like everyone else, have sex like everyone else, have kids like everyone else and get divorced like everyone else. Like those outside of the Church we have dysfunctional relationships, are emotionally scarred and make bad choices. In addition, we eat too much, get drunk, flirt and have multiple sexual partners – all like everyone else. We also have lots of fun. In fact, it often seems that being entertained is our highest priority, just like everyone else.

Is all this OK, or has something gone terribly wrong?

There is nothing new in believers looking and acting the same as the world around them. The problem has been around from the beginnings of Christianity. Paul had to spell it out to the early Greek converts:

*"I meant that you are not to associate with anyone who claims to be a believer yet indulges in sexual sin, or is greedy, or worships idols, or is abusive, or is a drunkard, or cheats people. Don't even eat with such people"* [1]

Paul was saying that if someone claiming to be a believer didn't reform their ways, then we should not get involved with them. We seem to be increasingly blurring these boundary lines.

In the West, Christianity has had a pretty good shot at shaping the society in which we live. We are the inheritors of hundreds of years of Christian heritage.

In Europe, social and political structures were founded on Christian ethos and values. Monastic orders all around Europe provided not just a prayer base for the known world, but also health care and education to the communities in which they lived. The reformation changed the entire political map of Europe, creating both Protestant and Catholic countries (of course some adopted the new religion only for political ends or, in the case of Henry VIII, to further their marital ambitions). Christian pioneers emigrated from Europe to what is now the USA to found new colonies so that their persecuted Christian sects could survive in freedom – something that is still a founding principle of America. The history of humanity is littered with Wesleys, Wilberforces, Nightingales and Theresas who pioneered, reformed and preached to change the world we live in.

❧

So we have attempted to make a difference to our world. We still do.

Millions of believers continue to attempt to make a difference. I recognize this, so don't think that I have some pessimistic view of the Church in the West, because I don't. My rhetoric is not intended to undermine the saints who are making a difference. My hope is to speak prophetically to the slumbering giant of the Church – that part of us that has allowed itself to lapse into a self-satisfied coma of indulgence and indifference.

I could cite hundreds of examples of mission and service activities that are making a huge impact in society, from the homeless feeding programs sponsored by churches all over the world, to the volunteer groups of believers that roam the streets of UK towns praying for and supporting drunken revellers. In my own town of Bath, UK, believers have fed the homeless with soup and sandwiches every day for 20 years! So making a difference, of course, we are.

But we still have a problem with our distinctiveness. Doing worthwhile things like the above is good, but it is not the essence of being distinctive. In the words of my fictional angel, "They all look the same!" You don't need to be a believer to do good works. For all the initiatives run by Christians treating people with drug addictions, for instance, there are many more secular programs. Believers don't have the monopoly on being "nice" or philanthropic. As I step back and look at our Christian world, I'm not convinced we look much different from those around us.

Take my town for example. I lead one of the larger, more prominent churches in the town. We own the largest auditorium in the region. We have a staff and programs designed to heal people's hurts, to teach people spiritual truth and to equip people to reach others. But if I zoom out and view this dispassionately for a moment, what difference do we bring to our area? If we were to disappear overnight, what effect would it have on our city?

If I was to be positive and optimistic I would hope that we would be missed. But it would probably be a momentary, "Oh dear, that's sad." It's the sort of comment people make when a 90 year old distant relative dies. You are sad, of course, but you accept that the inevitable has happened and you won't lose any sleep over it. Isn't that the attitude of our society to the Church? We're a bit sad for the loss, but we're not going to lose any sleep over its demise!

## In decline

There are those that feel that Christian Europe (or the Christian West) is in a terminal state of decline. Statistics seem to suggest a continued gradual decline in church affiliation and attendance at Sunday services. We have a generation of under 35's that really have no connection with church. They don't see it as offering anything of spiritual substance to society, or even offering any cultural or social benefit.

What goes on in the head of the average non-religious visitor to one of our great cathedrals? They are historically interesting perhaps (or boring), architecturally impressive, culturally quaint (an American said this), but by and large the impression is probably that the Christian distinctive is determined by a past that has no bearing on the present. Christianity occupies a cultural territory that is part of our living heritage and adds colour to our social structures, but is actually not really very important.

In the mind of the average non-believer, Christians are something akin to opera buffs: they get a "high" out of something that is totally inaccessible for most people; they go to a huge building, specially designed for the event, sit through a three hour performance delivered in a language the majority of people don't understand and it feeds their soul. Afterwards they discuss the performance, the key participants and celebrities, then go home raving about how wonderful it all is. (For a non-opera buff, the most wonderful thing may well be the gin and tonic in the interval to fortify them for the next instalment!) The whole thing costs a lot of money and people pay a fortune to engage in this activity. Is it relevant to society? Opera buffs will tell you that it is.

Why do we as a society keep it going? Because it is part of our rich heritage. It doesn't matter that it is elitist, it is part of our culture in the west. Every so often someone makes it accessible by bringing out a big opera star to sing *Nessun Dorma* at the opening of the World Cup, then everyone gets excited about it (unless you are Italian, in which case opera is as normal as breathing). See the similarities with church as it is perceived in our society? It culturally enriches society that prayers are said in Britain's Parliament, or that Scout groups go to church parades, or that Bishops have seats in the House of Lords, or that candlelit midnight masses fill churches up and down the country on Christmas Eve. We would miss our traditions based on Christian events.

Nevertheless, if there is evidence that this type of Christianity is in slow decline simply because it is an anachronism, a reflection of a past moral age, then decline it probably should. Even as I write this I am struck by the vivid truth that Christians do so much good, have so much history, have achieved so much, but are we the dying elderly relative of our society. We will be missed because we have always been there, but in the eyes of most we don't have much use any more; the duties we perform will be replaced by the fitter and younger, with new ideas and new ways of doing things.

"New" churches have a similar problem. We were founded in the last 40 years when radical pioneering believers felt the call to leave the established Church to pursue a new expression of Holy Spirit New Testament Church. The result was the planting of thousands of churches and a new movement of Spirit-filled churches. Decades later, leaders of this radical movement are more concerned with the management structures of staff, pension arrangements, building programmes and the structure of worship services than the hard edge of pioneering the kingdom. Inside I scream, "No, no, no!" Have we sold out to fit in? Have we matured and mellowed like all middle-aged people and lost the radical adventure of youth? Why don't I just speak up? Well my desire to be polite, be accepted and yes, to fit in, means that I sit silently while my inner radical is shouting and making a fuss! Like the bully in the school playground, the new person in a group, the youth that commits a crime, the new work colleague who doesn't know what they are doing - we all just want to be accepted and fit in!

## David was distinctive

I'm not suggesting we should be troublemakers in our communities and go around generally irritating our neighbours, but we do need to find ways to be distinctive and different. I have met some very irritating believers (if you know me and are reading this then I don't mean you!), people who stand on street corners and shout biblical truth in a meaningless way; people who don't know when is a good time or a bad time to share what they are feeling; people who manifest the Holy Spirit louder and bigger than anyone else in the room! However, despite their obviously irritating downside, I have to admit to harbouring a secret admiration for their disregard of how they appear to others. To be so passionate, so consumed, so given over to God is surely laudable, even if they are at times a little misguided.

King David in the Bible dancing in public dressed only in his CK boxers[2] is a classic example of the ridiculous[3]. Here is the highly respected and sought after anointed King of Israel, returning to the capital city bringing the ark of the covenant home with shouting, music and dancing. Most kings then and now would walk respectfully behind such a venerated object, but David believed he was honouring God with his actions. After all, the Israeli nation believed that this was "God in a box", the very presence of God contained within this sacred golden cask. It had just proved its power by killing poor old Uzzah who had tried to stop it from falling in the mud! Here was David looking like a complete buffoon, dancing and shouting like a court jester. No wonder his wife was completely disgusted. Husbands will be only too familiar with "the look" they get from their wives when they are doing something embarrassing! I get "the look" frequently, normally when I am being a buffoon, making everyone laugh (the showman in me) or singing Gilbert & Sullivan ditties for my own amusement. It happens when I start, "I am the very model of a modern major general" from Pirates of Penzance and might even elicit a full blast "Stewart!". Though I persist, I soon know when the joke has passed and the humour evaporated. What's worse is that my four daughters have learnt to do " the look" and join in with their mother – though secretly I think they all enjoy it!

Michal (David's wife and daughter of Saul, the previous king) gave David "the look" out of the window and subsequently an ear bashing when he got home. "What did you think you were up to? You are supposed to be the King! You were shamelessly exposing yourself to the servant girls like any vulgar person would. Have you no shame? You have embarrassed me!" She was pretty upset and wanted to hide. That's why she stayed upstairs and observed the whole sordid episode from her bed-room window.

But it is David's response that gets me. When I sing my out of fashion Victorian songs I normally reply, "I'm not embarrassed,

I'm just having a bit of fun." David, however, says, "I was dancing before the Lord. It wasn't meant for you or the servant girls. Do you know what? I am prepared to look more ridiculous, more silly, to humiliate myself, to be a complete fool if it means that I give the Lord God the honour He deserves." David, the respected ruler of his people, wasn't worried about what he "looked" like; his only concern was expressing the thing that was in his heart - its called worship!

I think this very simple story about David tells us something about what this book is all about. David was prepared to make himself a complete joke for the sake of the presence of God. He was prepared to do whatever it took to honour the presence of God. He has captured the distinctive that set him apart. He didn't value his position in society or his national identity at that moment; he valued the presence of God above all things. Paul, the apostle, put it like this:

*"I once thought these things were valuable, but now I consider them worthless because of what Christ has done."* [4]

He was referring to his pedigree, his academic ability, his sharp intellect, his standing in society. How can you get to a point in your life where all that you have worked for, all that you have built up, all the respect that you have gained is seen as worthless? Paul goes on,

*"Yes, everything else is worthless when compared with the infinite value of knowing Christ Jesus my Lord. For his sake I have discarded everything else, counting it all garbage so that I could gain Christ and become one with him."*

I am more than a little challenged by Paul's all out, committed, sold-out sentiment. These are not just words. Paul lived it!

## Sold out

How do we get to such a place where we are prepared to do whatever it takes to follow Jesus? Can we be that sold out? Do we want to be that sold out? Are we prepared to put our reputation, our desires, our dreams on the line? Do we regard all our achievements as "garbage" when compared to the opportunity to "know" the God of Gods? Truthfully, I would like to think that I can say "Yes!" But if I were to search my heart with piercing eyes, I think that I would fall short of such lofty sentiment.

We spend so much of our time engaged in self-improvement. Education is often our highest priority. In Africa it is amazing to see well turned out, clean children in their smart school clothes, leaving a tin shed of a home in the mud. Their parents know that to break the cycle of poverty their children must be educated at all costs. Similarly, in parts of the UK parents will move house just to get their children into the "best" school in the area. We spend our time raising our expectations of life and consequently our standard of living. Most parents want more for their children than they had for themselves - it is a natural, parental desire. Our aim and purpose in life is to raise the game for ourselves and our offspring, to go further, do better, earn more, achieve much. It is this attitude that has created the "body beautiful" culture we live in. Self improvement means to look better, because beautiful people have more opportunities in life – brains *and* beauty, the ideal combination. Men and Women have to look a certain way. Women need to fit into a size 8, have the right sized breasts, have their hair the way that *Hello Magazine* dictates. Men need to have the physique of a Greek god or at least be the rugged adventurer! So much energy, money and time spent on a pursuit that actually doesn't matter all that much.

Can you imagine then, if we counted our academic degree, our good looks and beauty, our stylish attire as "garbage" compared with someone far greater? Paul is of course trying to make a point. He used his position, his influence, his natural leadership skills, his zeal, his intellect to incredible use for the sake of the Gospel. Half the New Testament was written by him or was about him, so we would be poorer in our understanding of the early days of Christianity and the basic teaching of the faith without his powerful influence. But the issue for Paul was one of priority. He had found a treasure of so much worth that everything else paled into insignificance - it was this treasure that had become his distinctive.

## The pearl paradigm

Jesus is in story mode. The disciples have got used to the riddles that He tells: you ask Jesus a question and He comes up with a clever little saying that has you scratching your head for days after. This is one of those rare days when Jesus is actually explaining one of His parables. He has just finished explaining the story of the sower and the seed[5] when He launches into a number of other stories, one after the other. No sooner have the disciples got their heads around the sower tale than Jesus hits them with the wheat and weeds story, then the mustard seed, then the yeast ... Ah, stop! Let me get my mind around what you have just said! But then Jesus sneaks in another story: the one about hidden treasure![6]

In this parable Jesus compares the Kingdom of Heaven to buried treasure (you can all go, "Ha har!" like a pirate at this point) hidden in a field (a desert island would be better). Paraphrasing a little, the man, lets call him Jack (to carry on the pirate theme), finds a box of gold coins, rubies and diamonds and gets very excited. He has found something incredible. The trouble is, the land is owned by someone else and if they knew there was treasure on it, they would not sell it. So Jack finds the owner, let's call him One-eyed Black Jim (OK, I'm getting a bit carried away with *Pirates of the Caribbean* theme now) and buys the deeds to the land. Jack literally sells his house, his ship, everything he has because he knows the treasure is worth a fortune. He could buy a bigger house and a bigger ship!

Straight on the heels of this story, Jesus backs it up with a antique story[7]. An antiques dealer is at an auction and spots a rare pearl necklace. It is simply amazing, made from beautiful fresh water pearls, the largest he has ever seen. The dealer is completely intoxicated by the necklace and it has a spell-like hold on him. He can't resist it, he just has to have it. But the auction reserve price is £200,000. He works out he can buy, but only if he sells his flat, his car, and all his other antiques. He would be completely wiped out, but at least he will have the pearl necklace, and to him it is priceless!

What do these stories tell us? The distinctive of the Christian faith is not found in our good works, in our mission, or in our love of each other. It is not located in the influence we bring to bear on our communities, the homeless projects we run, or the youth groups, kid's clubs or elderly lunches. Nor is it in our healing centres or ministry initiatives. No, we count them all as rubbish compared to something far greater, far more priceless. The treasure island parable makes some sense. Jack could at least use the treasure to buy so much more than he ever had - a bigger ship, a grander mansion. Sure, he had to risk something to gain something, but it was worth the risk. But the antique dealer story makes no sense at all. He was completely infatuated with the pearl necklace and when he had sold all his assets what would he have? Nothing but a beautiful necklace (though what a necklace!) "What is the point in that?" would be the natural and pretty sensible response of some of Jesus' disciples. Is this Kingdom of Heaven worth all the risk, the trouble, worth wrecking our life's achievements for?

This is our dilemma. Is this Kingdom that Jesus spent His ministry on earth introducing, worth it? We know what the right answer is ("doh!"): of course it is worth it. But put your pious answer to one side. You are not impressing anyone because you are reading this on your own! This is the searching question that penetrates the core of our beings. This is the question that leaves us feeling naked before our God. This is the life-changing, radical question that will turn us upside down and inside out. The rational, academic, logical, practical, sensible answer is *it can't be worth the risk*, not for successful, affluent western believers. The treasure chest answer demands a slightly risky response based on the Bible's sowing and reaping concept: we invest in something and God blesses us in return. But the parable of the pearl necklace presents a deeper dilemma. To risk our all for something that is so priceless, so precious, something that we will never part with or sell once we have it, is beyond credibility for any sane believer.

But that's what this book is all about. The insane pursuit of the presence of God; a journey to find out what the very essence of the Church is all about; to find out what distinguishes us and differentiates us from all the other people on the face of the planet. I am feeling decidedly uncomfortable now; feeling as if my cosy life is going to be disrupted by something that is outlandish. I think I have gone some way to discovering the treasure island truth of the Kingdom, a Kingdom that costs everything, but delivers even more. I can say that after 30 years of being a believer, I think I get the treasure island paradigm. It undergirds serving, financial giving, the whole ethos of being a believer. But the pearl paradigm is a different matter. Selling out and selling all to get something that has an indeterminate outcome is a very different matter. Something that has infinite value, that can never be parted with, but will cost us *everything* – that is a dilemma.

Welcome to the pursuit of the Presence – the paradigm of the pearl. We are called to be Pearl Hunters!

## Endnotes

1. 1 Corinthians 5:11
2. Actually, it was a linen ephod which is a priestly garment, but underwear sets the right comical outrageous tone for the event.
3. 2 Samuel 6
4. Philippians 3:7-8
5. Matthew 13:1-23
6. Matthew 13:44
7. Matthew 13:45

# CHAPTER 2

# "Go With Us"

*"Then Moses said, 'If you don't personally go with us, don't make us leave this place. How will anyone know that you look favourably on me—on me and on your people—if you don't go with us? For your presence among us sets your people and me apart from all other people on the earth."* [8]
—Moses, speaking to God

Recently the media in the UK got hold of a scandal regarding MP's expense claims and really went for it. Of course, the general public joined in and began to moan and gripe about the fact that MP's were claiming for everything from second homes to toilet rolls, dog food to duck houses. As I write, the issue still rumbles on and the media has been relentless and savage. The consequence has been a chastised and dispirited House of Commons and an outpouring of anger from Mr General Public. Politicians are, of course, very concerned about what Mr GP thinks on all matters, because therein lies the source of their power! As an armchair politician myself, my mixed emotions on the matter have ranged from shouts of "Silly MP's to get themselves into this mess" to "Why can't the media just leave them alone?" Other voices have been less conciliatory, with shouts of "Off with their heads!" For several weeks it has felt like a chapter out of Alice in Wonderland.

## The desire for the authentic

But after calming down somewhat, what is my overriding reaction? I believe Mr GP's animated and angry response is yet another manifestation of his/her desire for authenticity. Instinctively we don't like hypocrisy. We can't stand it when someone tells us to do one thing, but does another himself. We expect a higher standard of behaviour from those who seek to lead us. We are outraged at failed bank bosses who take huge bonuses and pensions on leaving a business they destroyed. We are incensed with news of a social worker who fails to protect a child, a priest caught molesting a child, a lawyer on the fiddle, a doctor caught in a compromising situation with a patient. It is no surprise that (particularly) the tabloid media in the UK pick up on these stories with an exposé and we, Mr GP, lap up the gossip because if nothing else, it feeds our demand for something real and authentic.

The pursuit of all things spiritual is on the rise in our society. Finally, people are beginning to question whether meaning can be found in material things and are beginning to pursue "spiritual" solutions. It is part of the quest for the authentic, to find reality, to find meaning. Don't get the impression that there is a wholesale rejection of all things materialistic and hedonistic – not at all. This is a pick-n-mix spirituality that allows us to choose the sort of authentic experience we want. We can have just enough spiritual experience to satisfy us and still return to the pleasurable side of life. Not that everyone is like that, there are many who are pursuing spirituality full on and take on a morality much the same as Christians would. In my city I am involved in a "faith group" that has a voice to the city council.

In this setting I have conversations with Muslims, Jews, Bahis – you would be amazed at the unity we have when it comes to social or moral issues.

Is there a demand for authentic Christianity in this quest for truth? Some observers say that Christianity is on the sidelines, that it is no longer seen as the destination of the spiritually hungry, that church is no longer spiritually valid. I heard of one such conversation between a spiritually-seeking young woman and a Christian. The Christian asked her why she didn't go to church. Her reply was, "Why would I find anything spiritual in church?" I wonder how widespread this sentiment is – that the Church has little resources to meet our spiritual search?

On the other hand, churches get full at Christmas and Easter. "Charismatic/Pentecostal" churches are growing (mainly thanks to Africa and China) and there is enough good news to say that we are not completely dead in the water. I was at a summer camp this year where 11,000 Christians gathered for a week of worship and teaching (we were just one of many in the UK) and *The Independent* reported the event as "Glastonbury for God", so something is happening! What I think *is* dead or dying is church that is stale, overly wordy, finger wagging, lifeless, boring, dreary, out of date, Sunday-centred, and has little relevance to normal living. To be honest it is about time too. I would be very happy to conduct the funeral service for such churches! Many believers have become disaffected, disenchanted and disconnected from churches that don't change, have overly controlling leadership and have lost the life of the Holy Spirit. In a desperate attempt to find some energy and life they have either opted out of church altogether, preferring a private version of faith (I don't believe you can have a private faith and still be called a Christian), given up on faith altogether or started up their own expression of church which ticks the boxes of no-control and realism.

## Churches near death!

The great thing about dead churches, rather than dying ones, however, is that they leave room for the God of the resurrection! My prayer is that the funeral service for many of our nation's churches will be interrupted by a tap from inside the coffin and that new life will return to churches once thought to be on their last legs! Many churches that are at the end of their lifespan have lost the dynamic that their founding fathers had. Rather than staying on the cutting edge of faith, pursuing something in God, they have reverted to "Museum mode", merely keeping what they have as a memorial to their founders. The best memorial we can build to our founders, however, is not to be true to the rules that were put in place, the statements of orthodoxy, the buildings that were created, the structures of church government – but rather to be true to the fire that burned in their bellies, that caused them to sacrifice their lives for the truth of the Gospel. The founders of these movements had the spirit of David – they were prepared to look ridiculous in order to pioneer something fresh and true to the Scriptures.

The Quakers[9] were founded in the UK around 1650 as a radical, Holy Spirit movement that clashed with the established Church of the day. Its founder, George Fox[10], got a revelation of the reality and authority of Christ in the individual believer. This brought him into conflict with the authority structures of the established Church. Church to Fox was not about the ceremony, the building, the professional priest, but rather Christ expressing Himself through the individual believer. Fox was abrupt, outspoken and desperately earnest in his views. In short he was authentic and this appealed to huge numbers of people, particularly as healings, miracles and charismatic phenomena accompanied his ministry. On one occasion Fox prayed and, "… the Lord's power was so great that the house seemed to be shaken. When I had done, some of the professors said it was now as in the days of the Apostles, when the house was shaken where they were."[11]

Stories of shoulders getting healed, the lame walking, discernings in the Spirit, speaking in tongues were all recorded in his *Book of Miracles*. This was a powerful move of God. But where are the Quakers today? Recently their council agreed to allow the marriage of homosexual couples in their buildings!

I humbly and without a heart that seeks to judge feel compelled to point out the sad state of many of our church movements that are falling or have fallen into a similar sad state. The purpose of this will become clear. In it all, my hope is to see revival and restoration to all denominations and movements, for us to be true to the inspirational stories of our founders and to see the power of Christ displayed in these historic movements. Don't get offended, just call on the name of the Lord Jesus!

The Methodists were an incredible force in the UK, restoring a passion for God and sweeping the fire of revival across Britain. One theory advanced not long after the French Revolution was that Methodism was a major force which prevented Britain undergoing a similar bloody revolution from a monarchy to a republic.[12] John Wesley[13], the horse riding evangelist and movement creator had his heart "strangely warmed"[14], which started a ferocious fire of the Holy Spirit all across Britain. He found himself laughing uncontrollably, being healed of his own sickness miraculously, and speaking in tongues. He was accused of "inferring" by a "Mr Church", of all people, that people were "cured" under his ministry. He agreed, saying,

"As it can be proved by abundance of witnesses that these cures were frequently (indeed almost always) the instantaneous consequences of prayer, your inference is just. I cannot, dare not, affirm that they were purely natural. I believe they were not. I believe many of them were wrought by the supernatural power of God."[15]

Methodism took hold in Britain. "The social changes which accompanied this revival of faith, especially in the poorer segments of society, were immense. The drinking dens which sowed violence and poverty at the heart of working communities were closed down, not by the authorities but for a simple lack of trade. Pit ponies, which dragged wagons of coal in mining villages of industrial England, could no longer understand their drivers who had ceased to curse and swear at them!"[16] Methodism, if there is ever a need for the fire that you carried in your founding, it is now!

Let's bring this up to date with my own movement – the Charismatic movement of the late 1960s, under the direction and leadership in the UK of Arthur Wallis, Bryn Jones and Gerald Coates. These churches were birthed out of a yearning for a more authentic expression of New Testament Church. The established churches seemed to have lost any power and freedom of the Holy Spirit, so these pioneers were led of God was to establish something in houses. Let me point the finger at myself. I inherited the leadership of one of the early churches in that movement. It is forty-one years since we were founded in an apartment in Bath. But as I gaze on the "house church movement" as it became known, I see as many churches who have lost their fervour, their passion for the Holy Spirit and are now on the edge of the charismata. We have turned from pioneers to settlers, become the guardians of big churches, programmes and buildings. We wrestle with organisational issues and have paid staff to manage. We are concerned with cash flow, with our media output, with our DVD and book sales, ensuring the numbers of our next conference are sufficient to make a profit. We turn our attention to keeping our largish congregations amused and entertained, keeping their attendance up and, more importantly, their tithe intact.

## Can you hear the cry?

Can you hear the groan of the Spirit in what I am saying? Movements birthed out of spiritual awakening seem to end up taking a wrong turn. They start well – they are exciting, radical and passionate – but time erodes the founding tablets of stone; the fire becomes an ember smouldering until it eventually becomes burnt out ash – nothing remaining of its once glorious heat. All of which brings me to the cry of Moses to his God at the start of this chapter.

*"Then Moses said, 'If you don't personally go with us, don't make us leave this place. How will anyone know that you look favourably on me—on me and on your people—if you don't go with us? For your presence among us sets your people and me apart from all other people on the earth."* [17]

This cry is so real right now for the Church. An anguished shout of "God we need you now", a scream for help arises from the gut of the intercessor.

Perhaps a bit of context for these verses would be helpful.

## Moses' story

Moses had just led in triumph and with great victory the people of God out of Egypt, the place of captivity. It was a pretty monumental escape entailing plagues and miracles. Even the angel of death makes a dramatic appearance. In essence, the stubborn ruler of Egypt who knew Moses as a brother (if you believe the Hollywood *Prince of Egypt* version of the story) held out for as long as he could – he didn't want his complete work-force leaving the country -- but eventually he let them go, only to change his mind and chase them with his crack troops into the Red Sea, which was miraculously being held back like a curtain, to be closed over the pursuing enemy army. Signal end of Pharaoh, end of Egypt's control. This is also a great picture of Christian baptism, the end of the old and beginning of the new. But the free people of God were now triumphant and in the desert buffer zone, singing the number one hit about their destination – the Promised Land.

The old behaviour of captivity didn't take long to show itself, however. I suppose bad habits die hard. With nothing to eat and nothing to drink for a million people there was a bit of a problem for dear old Moses (who didn't even want the job of leader in the first place). So there followed more miracles: heaven-sent bread, heaven-sent quails and fresh water fountains springing out of rocks, all produced by the Provider God for His people. Moses had promised God to return to Mount Sinai (more of that in the next chapter) to worship, sacrifice and receive the next lot of orders from his Commander-in-Chief. They arrive, make camp at the foot of the mountain, Moses gets some new instructions called the Ten Commandments and a load of detail about a tent for God, which keeps him up the mountain for a long time. The people of God get irritated by the delay, so decide to take matters into their own hands and make a golden cow and worship that instead of God, at least until Yahweh shows Himself again. Perhaps they genuinely thought Moses was a goner, burnt to a crisp by the power of God?

God interrupts his meeting with Moses to tell him about what the people are doing. God exclaims that He is ready to kill the whole lot of them and start again with Moses. Moses appeases God and comes down the mountain incensed that his people have broken the first commandment in the most flagrant way. He drops the stone tablets which God Himself had inscribed with His finger, pulls the abominable gold statue from its place of honour and throws it into the fire. He gets Aaron (his bother, priest and spokesman) by the scruff of the neck, who mutters something like, "Don't you think you are overreacting Moses?" and realises his lax leadership has let

everyone get out of control. Moses then challenges the people
to stand behind him if they are on the Lord's side, which the
Levite tribe instantly do, and to those who have chosen God he
tells them to slaughter all the revellers, regardless of whether
they are brothers, friends or neighbours. 3,000 get massacred
that day. Tragic, but better than everyone which was God's
original suggestion!

What about the aftermath? What to do with such a rebellious
and outrageous people? God was pretty clear with Moses: *"I
will erase the name of everyone who has sinned against me"*[18] and
He followed it up with a plague. The people mourned, they
realised that they had gone too far, this was serious! God could
not presence Himself with His people now. The very proximity
of His presence to His people would kill them off. *"If I were to
travel with you for even a moment, I would destroy you."*[19]   In
short, they were completely stuffed!

Moses had the practice of going regularly to the special tent
he had erected to meet with God. People would stand at the
entrances to their tents and watch him go in and have a face-
to-face with God. The column of cloud that clearly demonstrated
that God was around hovered over the door of the tent while
He and Moses were in conference.

On one of these occasions, in the aftermath of the slaughter
and plague, Moses has the conversation quoted at the beginning
of the chapter. His argument is that God is telling him to carry
on the journey to the Promised Land, but clearly God won't be
with them in the way He has been up to now. God has said He
will destroy the people if He goes anywhere near them. The
presence of God and sin do not mix. So Moses calls in a favour
from God: "God, if I am so favoured by you, then I need you
to go with us" (my translation). God replies, "Of course I will
go with you, you are going to be blessed, I will go with you
personally." Moses is going to be just fine, he will be blessed in

his life, his descendents will be blessed, God is on his case. Now look at this extraordinary act of leadership and compassion. He had developed such a relationship with God that he could conduct this sort of conversation. Remember, this is the God who spoke from the mountain, opened the waters, sent the angel of death, sent a plague ... Moses talks with God as if He were his mate – that's because He was! "You have got to go with US God, not just me. In fact, I am not leaving this desert, this place of encounter, until you agree to go with US. How will anyone in the land you've promised we'll inherit know that you are our God unless you actually go with US? People will only know that your favour is on us if you actually go with US." Moses got it. He realised that any further travels without the presence of God were a waste of time.

Moses had got to the point in his life where he realised that it was just not worth going on, not worth doing anything more, not worth taking another step, unless God PERSONALLY went with his people. Moses had set out to release a nation from slavery and take them to the Promised Land that had been set out in an oath to Abraham. This was still his aim. Why go on and try to take the territory unless God was with them? It was great for Moses to have a personal experience of God, but Moses knew his destiny and connection with the people of God was far more important. He had read the yearning, grieving heart of God which longed for His very own people. God, the essence of community (Father, Son and Holy Spirit) wanted to be in community with His created beings. The powerful God who created man to rule over the earth, who was created to have a relationship with the divine, had in His heart the desire of unity with man. Moses knew this, he was God's friend after all. God knew that His presence, His holiness, His glory would kill humanity in its sin-infested state, so He could not presence Himself with them, but Moses recognised that his friendship was enough to avert this disaster. He had penetrated the heart of God and was operating in something called "faith" [20] when he pleaded with God to PERSONALLY go with them as a people and not give up on them.

Moses realised that it was only the presence of God which distinguished him and his people from all the other people on the face of the earth. In his developing relationship with God he had learned the truth of the pearl paradigm: the pearl of great price was knowing God personally. The people were not the models of holiness, nor had they the moral fibre to resist evil, or stop moaning, or generally live like the people of God, but when the presence of God was with them they were able to be set apart, be different, distinctive.

God agrees and Moses then says, *"Show me your glory."*

Paul wrote, *"Don't you know that you yourself are God's temple and that God's Spirit lives in you?"* [21] and *"Your body is a temple of the Holy Spirit … you are not your own."* [22] – so why don't we live like it? These are not some theoretical, theological concepts, they are supposed to be reality. Moses got this truth, how else was he be able to stand in the presence of God? He operated by faith in the Saviour who had yet to be revealed (don't get me started on God being outside of time, and Old Testament saints being justified by faith in the Christ that was to come – that is the New Testament reality). Yet we who are in Christ and stand as friends of God have the continual presence of God with us, but we squander this treasure!

This is the pearl paradigm: a realisation that nothing much matters unless the presence of God goes with us. Unless we are marked by the presence of God, unless we are guided by the Holy Spirit, unless we are covered, directed and fed by the Holy Spirit, what is the point on going any further?

The answer for a decaying Church in the West is this: get more of the presence of God! The secret to reviving dying

institutional Church is: *pursue the presence of God.* Our profit
motive will be blown away by the presence, our dull ritual will
be set on fire by the presence, our lost fervour and lost passion
will be found in the presence. The distance that has crept into
our lives will be narrowed, the silence of God will be given a
voice, the touch of God will be felt by the presence. Like moving
from the black and white of Kansas to the Technicolor of Oz,
the presence of God brooding over His people makes all the
difference.

We are looking for difference, for distinctiveness, for something that marks out the people of God. It isn't mission, it isn't
social justice, it isn't authentic community, it isn't anything
that we do or any programme that we run – it has to be the
unfettered, fire-like presence of God.

When you taste this presence, when you feel this presence,
when you are exposed to this presence it will burn something
on the inside of you. When you encounter the authentic, real,
powerful, mighty, loving presence of God, you are branded
forever. You will experience the fire that branded Finney,
Whitefield, Wesley, Edwards, Fox, Luther, Anthony, Paul, Jesus
– you will just want more. Like Moses you will see the futility
of doing anything, going anywhere, saying anything without
the enduring, sustaining presence of God. It is this presence,
this Holy Spirit that is worth selling out for. It is the pearl of
the Kingdom of God – that's what we are pursuing.

## Endnotes

8. Exodus 33:15-16
9. Officially know as the Religious Society of Friends
10. George Fox 1624-1691
11. Rufus M. Jones, ed, George Fox; An Autobiography (Philadelphia, PA : Ferris and Leach, 1919) p90
12. The theory was originally proposed by Elie Halevy, A History of the English People 1815, (1913) trans, Watkins & Barker (Harcourt Brace, 1924)
13. 1703-1791
14. The words Wesley used when writing about his conversion.
15. Eddie L. Hyatt, 2000 years of Charismatic Christianity, Charisma House 2002 p103
16. Phil Anderson, The Lord of the Ring, A Journey in search of Count Zinzendorf; Survivor/Kingsway 2006 p195 - this is a great account of Count Zinzendorf the founder of the Moravians.
17. Exodus 33:15-16
18. Exodus 32:33
19. Exodus 33:5
20. Hebrews 11:23-29 highlights the actions of Moses as operating by faith.
21. 1 Corinthians 3:16
22. 1 Corinthians 6:19

# Experiencing Encounter

*The train is heard pulling out of the station. Laura rushes to get one last glimpse of her lover. The lights of a passing train light up Laura's destitute face. Now she will have to return to the dullness of her suburban life; the months of emotional adventure are over.*

These are the final moments of David Lean's classic love story *Brief Encounter*. The film conveys all the emotion of a love that cannot be. A couple – both married with children – long to be together, but they can't. Alec and Laura meet in a railway station and this briefest of meetings turns into a love affair which eventually ends when Alec takes a job in South Africa. They represent middle class morality, stuck in a crisis of wanting something they cannot have.

I don't agree with the morality of the film or support the idea that it's okay to have a fling while you are married. What interests me here is the enduring fascination the world has with a love story built on an encounter. Something in the poetry of this film resonates with the human soul because it cries out for authentic love, the pursuit of our desires, our longing to have a chance meeting that changes everything. An encounter is more that just a meeting – it is an unexpected rendezvous leading to an adventure. The parties engage with each other and an exchange happens. Encounters do not leave us unmoved; they change us – forever.

Noel Coward, who wrote the play *Brief Encounter* was based on, did not intend any parallels to be made to faith or the pursuit of God, but I see many Christians who are like this couple. Put aside the morality issues for a moment and look at the metaphors. A couple find adventure and meaning in life by being together. The railway station – which under other circumstances would be dull and uninspiring – becomes a place of excitement as they continue to encounter one another passionately. But the happiness is short lived and one is left alone, bereft and with endless questions.

In the same way, many believers encounter the Living God with excitement. He brings them meaning and purpose, revealing the amazing scope of His divine love story to them. Yet, they end up feeling abandoned on the cold, station platform of life, the object of their affection moving into the distance. Belief in the divine lover seems far away; we feel let down. The evangelist's promise of "Come to Jesus and all your troubles will disappear" didn't work out as promised. The plans we made – the missions we would go on, the revivals we would see, the exploits we would do for Jesus – are a fading memory. All that lies in front of us is a humdrum life of morality without meaning, obedience to conventions. We attend church, we give our money, we say our prayers, we read our Bibles ... but the spark that once lit up our life is no longer there.

Surely, there must be more than this?

When I came to faith in my early teens I had an encounter with God. It gripped me in a way that I can only appreciate retrospectively. At the time there was nothing spectacular about my repentance and confession to Jesus of the all important words: "I make you Lord of my life" – as if the concept of Lordship had any real meaning to a fourteen year old. But I was drawn to the people of faith. My first encounter with God had been through His people. I couldn't put my finger on it, but I was attracted by the fact there was "something different" about them – there was a reality about them I liked. This second encounter, however, was different. Now I was speaking to God for myself, praying the prayer in faith and believing that my life would change as a result. Amazingly, change did happen. I experienced an emotional high – a feeling that I had done the right thing. I knew I was different. I now understand that I had become a new creation[23] and the only evidence of it was faith.

This was the beginning of my story. For some believers, their first encounter with God is the end of the story. They really do have a "brief encounter" with God, grasping something of His incredible love for them, but never doing anything with it. For me, that was not good enough. My God moment was enough to tell me that there was much more to this than a fleeting "feel good" moment. Since then I have come to realise that my encounter with God is an ongoing story, an everyday occurrence that turns the dull station waiting room of life into a place of excitement, emotion and adventure.

## Encounter should be normal

Leaving the funeral of their leader, two very disillusioned friends began the seven mile walk home. It had been a long week which had started well. They were part of the cavalcade that entered the city, the people honouring their leader with a ticker tape parade. But a week is a long time in politics. They did not think for a minute they would be attending his funeral by the end of it! As they walked and exchanged memories, they were joined by a stranger who seemed to have no clue about these momentous events. "Haven't your heard the news?" they asked. "No," replied the stranger, "what's happened?" The friends unburdened their hearts to him: "A prophet of our time ... incredible miracles ... he taught with such clarity ... how could they assassinate him?... we would have followed him to the grave!" But the story had an open ending! Other friends had told them that the dead hero's body had gone missing. Why, they didn't know. It made no sense. They were sad and confused.

All the time the stranger just listened. Then he began to talk. They noticed he was interesting, compelling even, easy to listen to. What he said made so much sense that excitement stirred inside their hearts. Three hours passed quickly and they reached home. The stranger made out that he was travelling further, but they pleaded with him to stay and have some food with them. He agreed. As the stranger picked up the fresh bread and tore it in half, he said a prayer of thanks. At that moment they realised – they had spent the afternoon with Jesus! Immediately he disappeared from sight.[24]

What I love about this story is that the resurrected Jesus revealed Himself in an ordinary way. No angelic trumpets, no glory shining from heaven, no radiant faces – He just walked, talked and ate food with his friends (a recurring biblical practice!). We have a tendency to look for and pursue the extraordinary, but most of us, most of the time, will encounter the Living God in the ordinary, everyday events that shape us. Don't think though, that these everyday moments of encounter are without significance. We look at our frequently mundane existence with the wrong eyes; we need to look at our lives through the lens of heaven to see the spiritual reality that exists.

Jesus sat down with His disciples for food – nothing spectacular about that. It was when He began to enact the "Lord's Supper" that the eyes of His friends were opened and the resurrected Jesus disappeared from sight. When the men looked at

Jesus with their natural eyes, they saw Him, but they didn't truly "see" Him. As soon as they saw the spiritual connection, however, they suddenly recognised Him, but then Jesus disappeared from physical sight. Like these men, how much of our "normal" day hides spiritual reality? We need our spiritual eyes to be opened to see beyond the mundane and grasp the spiritual reality. The Bible speaks about those who have entertained angels without actually knowing it.[25] We need to see with spiritual eyes!

## There's more

Though my story of becoming a Christian is a simple one – based on a simple decision – behind it lies the power-packed reality of spiritual regeneration. I made a small choice, but I was transformed into a new creation and began a journey. We may never experience a dramatic encounter with God, but this does not negate the reality of our encounter with Jesus Christ. Thomas the doubter believed when he saw the hands of Jesus, but if you believe without seeing tangible proof then you are blessed of God.[26]

The problem is that many believers stop here, after their initial encounter experience. Having come to Christ, they seem content with spiritually never seeing any further! I don't really understand why, but many people refer to their conversion experience as the *only* real encounter they every had with God. How strange , to experience a divine, life-changing event, and then never experience God again. I cannot believe in a God who abandons His children at birth – that does not sound like a God of love to me. Why would anyone follow a God who met them in a brief encounter and then left them to their own devices to live a life of monotonous sameness? Yet, so many people seem to have formed this view of God. They see God as a silent, distant Father, uninterested in their life.

This is, of course, not a true picture but a distortion of reality. God does not desire for us to have a one-off experience of Him to last us the rest of our lives. To think otherwise is as ridiculous as saying that my wife and I had a one-off experience on our wedding day, which should be sufficient to see us through the rest of our lives. No! Any meaningful relationship is an ongoing series of encounters, meetings and shared experiences. Why would we think relating to God would be any different? If we accept that He created us with needs and emotions, then we must accept the idea that we are created with an inbuilt need for relationship – and our core purpose is exactly that: to be in relationship with God!

The book of beginnings (Genesis) makes this very plain. First of all we see that God, three distinct persons in one, is in relationship with Himself – a concept that theologians have grappled with for centuries. Then we see man, Adam, created to bring order and rule to the world. God created man in His own image, literally replicating His very essence[27], with an innate desire to be in relationship, to be connected to the divine. God recognised that man needed to mirror this spiritual connection with a physical connection, so also created woman – a perfect match to satisfy the physical nature of man. So here we have man and woman in relationship – a reflection of the relationship that exists in the Trinity.

Once again, this relationship functions in the normality of life. It begins with God walking in the garden for a regular chat with his new, special creation.[28] There is no sense of distance between God and man, no silent treatment. Adam experienced an initial encounter with God when the divine breath was imparted to a pile of mud and chemicals. But after that we see the pattern of an everyday, normal, ongoing relationship. This is the way relationship is supposed to work! God is highly relational and man, His "replica" – another meaning for "image" is therefore relational too. No other creature on earth has a similar mental, emotional and spiritual makeup where relationships play such a big part.

Even after the expulsion from Eden, God still wants to relate to man – though the introduction of sin into the equation now makes relations much more complex, since God and sin don't mix. In fact, from Genesis onwards, the entire Bible narrative is concerned with God's efforts to restore His friendship with man.

## Dreaming and fighting

Jacob was a man who had a serious encounter with God. He was a pretty shifty character. Egged on by his mother, he conned his brother out of his inheritance and then had to run away to his Uncle, fearing that his brother would beat him senseless. But God took Jacob seriously, mainly because God takes His promises seriously, so while he was in transit to his relatives, Jacob encountered God properly for the first time.

The night was drawing in and Jacob realised he couldn't travel much further. He found some shelter by some rocks and began to set up camp. He set himself a fire and boiled up some stew. He was a pretty good chef; his game pie was so delicious that his brother swapped his inheritance for a slice. In fact, it was because of his game pie that he was on the run! He settled down for the night. Sleeping on the ground, he found a smooth rock to act as a pillow. He was the sort of outdoors guy people make TV programmes about.

That night he had an incredible dream. He saw an escalator coming down from heaven, the sort you see at airports or new stations. He was literally in Heaven's arrivals and departure lounge. It was a busy place, with angels going back and forth for assignments on earth. God spoke to Jacob from the top of the escalator: "I'm the Lord God, the same God your fathers worshipped. You are sleeping on the land that I have promised you. Your nation is going to grow and spread out. I'm going to watch out for you." Jacob woke up in a cold sweat, realising that he had been dreaming. It wasn't brought on by the game pie – God really had spoken to him. By now he must have been feeling terribly guilty about the previous week's deceptions.

During his encounter, God had literally opened up the sky to Jacob, drawn back the physical veil and allowed him to see into Heaven. It was a "dream", but dreams are a great way for God to intervene in our lives – after all, we can't argue with Him when we are asleep! The Church needs to recapture the role of dreams in God speaking to us, not abandon it as a "New Age" concept. Imagine the impact of Jacob seeing these warrior and messenger angels going about their business. "God is here and I didn't know it" was his exclamation. Such an encounter with God changes our perspective.

*"What an awesome place this is! It is none other than the **house of God**; the very gateway to heaven."* (Genesis 28:17)

This startling revelation that God wanted to protect and bless Jacob shook him to the core. Something in Jacob changed on this day. He realised that his father Isaac's stories of going up the mountain and nearly being sacrificed by Jacob's grand-father were true. His granddad was not exaggerating when he said that God had promised his descendants a land of their own. Before then Jacob had probably taken all this with a pinch of salt, but now his heart missed a beat as he saw the family stories about greatness and significance were actually true. Stealing his birthright from his brother now came into perspective. He was not simply tampering with a quaint family tradition – he was messing with God!

Encounter has that affect. It awakens us from the sleepiness of our lives, shakes us from seductive complacency and rocks us out of our tidy, ordered lives. That's why we need to cultivate encounter, to desire encounter, to be prepared to pursue it time and time again. God responds to our desire for encounter. He seems to come whenever people are really hungry for Him. I hear believers moan that contemporary Church is not like it was in New Testament times, with signs and miracles, but are we pressing in to see them? Are we hungry in our hearts and committed to an encounter lifestyle? Or do we expect to see miracles after just one prayer and an exciting church meeting?

Later on,[29] when Jacob is older and wiser (though still a bit manipulative) he has another night time encounter with God. On this occasion a mystery man fights Jacob all through the night. Jacob hangs on. He is a tenacious wrestler and will not give up. Eventually the man says he must leave, but Jacob insists on receiving a blessing. Over the years he has learned the value of a spoken blessing – something we can often dismiss as old fashioned, but is it? The man ends the fight by touching Jacob's thigh which is instantly wrenched out of its socket. He only touched Jacob, but it was a divine touch. Then he speaks a blessing: "You are now called Israel (meaning "God fights") because you have fought God and man and won."

What does it mean to be a fighter? The authority figures in our lives – our mothers, teachers and policemen – told us not to fight. It wasn't good Christian behaviour. But we need to learn to be fighters! We have become so wimpy in our faith, so impotent and boring! I am no physical fighter – put me in a boxing ring and I'd be out on the first punch – but God has made me a fighter. I am going to press in, push through the obstacles and make a difference. Life will throw plenty of muck at you, but if you have a Jacob spirit you will fight through it. We sanitise Christianity to be something reverent, quiet, meek and humble. But the faith I see in the Bible is earthy, pushy, vibrant and creative. Encounter, therefore, is not really about getting goose bumps in worship or falling over in the Spirit when someone prays for you. Encounter is about a radical touch, a power experience, something that leaves you different.

I like Jacob. Though he was scheming, crafty and slightly Machiavellian, he was also hungry, eager and a fighter! Even while he is making big mistakes he meets with God! He called the site of his supernatural wrestling match Peniel (meaning "face of God"). He acknowledged the mystery man as "God". He had encountered the very face of the Living God and somehow survived.

## Experience

Something odd has crept into our western evangelical Christian mindset. It is the distrust of experience – as though everything good and trustworthy in life is only logical and factual. Using our brains to apply rational thought and possessing an inquisitive nature is something that sets us apart from the rest of creation. It is one of the most distinguishing features of humanity. In fact, the acquisition of knowledge and growth through learning is vital to our culture. But why do we Christians have a downer on *experience*? It seems that today's good, Bible-believing Christians want everything to be proven to them, as if having to "prove" something means that it's true.

It has been said that a person with a theory will never be at the mercy of a person with an experience. I think we worry about basing our lives on experience (as well as knowledge) because we know there can be both good and bad spiritual experiences – those that are authentic, originating from God, and those that are demonic in origin. But we are so fearful of having a counterfeit spiritual experience that we throw out the authentic!

Sometimes, all we can say for sure is that we *know* we have encountered God. Trying to articulate the experience or prove its meaning is a sure way of killing its impact. Right now, as I write, it is late morning and I'm on holiday in Spain. I am looking out over the Mediterranean and a warm breeze is blowing in the shade of the veranda. To my right are the distant mountains merging into the clouds. I'm inspired and relaxed. Have I shared the moment, the experience? Now can I prove that this experience is real? Where do I start? Well, the temperature is 32°C, the time is exactly midday. I am in the North East of Spain about 100 miles north of Barcelona. It is the Day of Assumption and fireworks are going off in the nearby town. I am situated on a hill about 1/2 mile from the sea as the crow flies and about 300 metres above sea level. The sea has a temperature of .... are you bored yet? I'm bored just writing it. Who is interested in the minutiae, the detail of the experience? Isn't it better just to have the experience?

I don't want to have a go at biblical scholars, in fact my office is full of commentaries and biblical study books, but talk about sucking the life out of something! The problem with some (not all) exegesis is that it leaves us looking at something that has been dissected, but doesn't give us the whole meaning. When we dissect Scripture line by line, we lose so much of the whole. Though the Bible is utterly invaluable to us, by binding up Scripture into a leather-bound book, we have made a statement that says, "This is it!" Of course, I believe in the infallibility of God's Word, but our "this is it" statement has meant that many fail to understand the unfolding nature of revelation through an ongoing relationship with the Holy Spirit. The Bible is a record of the many amazing encounters God has had with His people – but He still wants us to encounter Him now! The story is still being written in and through our lives.

## Altar

I need to point out here that we can and should experience "encounter" with God through the Scriptures. It never ceases to amaze me how powerfully the Bible can speak into our lives. In all things we need to have balance, so we cannot be overly dependent on dreams and visions – we also need to be planted in Scripture to avoid going down a spiritual cul-de-sac. But those whose spiritual life is devoid of excitement and vibrancy need to cultivate a new hunger for encounter through experience – it cannot be all theory. Maybe it is time to climb onto the altar and say to God, "Here I am, Lord. I will not leave here until I have experienced something of You!" It doesn't matter whether it takes weeks or months for something to happen. Eventually, at the right time, God will show up. He can't help but respond to your heart cry.

After his wrestling match, Jacob went back to the place where he had his original God-encounter at Bethel. God had told him to go and build an altar there and make it his home.[30] This was the place where God responded to the desperate Jacob, promising His presence, the place of revelation. The idea of the altar is the simplest expression of the meeting place between God and man, the place of encounter. The altar only enters the biblical narrative after the fall of mankind, when the first family have been ejected from the garden. It embodies the idea of "sacrifice" in order to restore communication and relationship with God.

Cain and Abel brought their sacrificial offerings before God[31]. Though it does not say so explicitly, Scripture implies the use of an altar and we read of God's reaction to their respective offerings. After Noah had completed his sailing mission, the first thing he did was to build an altar and sacrifice some of his precious cargo.[32] God smelled the fragrance of sacrifice and that was enough to convince Him to never wash away society again. Abraham was given the hardest test when God asked him to sacrifice his son on an altar, which was given the name "The Lord will provide"[33] and the theme of God producing a substitute was introduced into history. Isaac had a God-encounter at Beersheba[34] where God made promises, so he built an altar to worship Him. Moses made an altar and called it the "Lord is my Banner"[35] celebrating the defeat of his enemies. Later the Lord asked him to build an altar at the foot of the mountain which God decided to inhabit with a glory fire and smoke.[36]

The altar represents sacrifice, promise, remembrance and revelation – the place where God meets with man; the place where man brings an offering; the place where God speaks out His promises and affection; the place where the triumphs and encounters are remembered in a physical place and where God reveals His heart to His people. It is the place where God deals with our sin, where we must go to surrender our lives. The altar is where God chooses to presence Himself, the point of personal transaction, the point of connection, the secret and holy place where you and God do business together.

*"I want you to show love, not offer sacrifices. I want you to know me more than I want burnt offerings."* —God, speaking through the prophet Hosea.[37]

Your altar may mean laying down something you cherish. Your altar may require you to set you heart on pilgrimage, following God's presence wherever He leads until you experience that encounter. Whatever it means for you, and whatever it takes, remember we are selling everything we have in order to acquire that of infinite value. God is searching our hearts. The stuff of life is incidental. It is the depth of our hunger and the determination of our heart to experience Him that will lead to the most meaningful type of encounter.

## Endnotes

23. Galatians 6:15
24. Luke 24:13-34
25. Hebrews 13:2
26. John 20:29
27. Genesis 1:27
28. Genesis 3:8
29. Genesis 32:22-32
30. Genesis 35:1
31. Genesis 4
32. Genesis 8:20
33. Genesis 22:14
34. Genesis 26:23
35. Exodus 17:15
36. Exodus 24:4
37. Hosea 6:6

# Obey

This year my eldest daughter got married. What a wonderful day! I blubbed the whole way through. One of the things that people watch for in a marriage ceremony is whether the bride will promise to "obey" or not. It is not at all fashionable to "obey". The cultural norm screams, "You can't tell me what to do!" Advertising constantly reinforces the rights of the individual. Companies pretend that "Everything we do is driven by you" to seduce us into thinking we actually matter to them.

In one sense, I am pleased that I live in a society where an individual's freedom is given value. The opposite is a dictatorial regime where we are told what to do when. I was recently in Russia, where hot water is pumped directly into people's homes from the power station, so they are not given the choice or responsibility to heat it themselves! During the winter (which in Russia is very long), no one can decide whether to turn the heating on or off – that decision is made by a power station official. After all, why should an ordinary person decide whether they are hot or cold? The State will decide for them. Such is the legacy of extreme communism where the needs of individuals are subsumed to the collective good.

Though we think of ourselves as living in a "free society" in the West, however, we cannot escape the giving and taking of orders. Obedience to certain rules and norms comes as part of life, despite what the media says to the contrary. Good parents tell their children what to do and expect obedience. Employers can't just offer suggestions to their employees, they have to give directions. Governments would fall apart if their laws are not complied with. Freedom is not found in the absence of boundaries, as some like to believe. Actually, freedom can be found in order.

Jesus understood the principle of freedom in obedience. He said, *"I only do what the father requires of me."*[38] He understood the will of His Father and wanted to do whatever His Father asked of Him. He didn't argue, He didn't doubt, He just obeyed. Why? Because He totally understood the nature of the Father. He recognised that the Father would not ask Him to do something that did not have a higher purpose or was not intrinsically good, even if that meant being obedient to death. Jesus went on to give His disciples this clear advice: *"You need to do the will of the Father to get into the Kingdom of Heaven."*[39] In other words, He told us to do what the Father says! John picked up on this theme and later wrote, *"Loving God means keeping his commands."*[40] So whether we like the word or not, obedience to God's commands is an important part of being His disciples.

## Getting orders!

I have discovered, both from experience and Scripture, that encounters are often times when we receive orders from God. In our ongoing journey with Him, He will at various times need to give us instructions He wants us to fulfil. Our initial encounters with God tend to be about Him revealing His character to us: He reveals Himself as Saviour when we come to Christ; later He reveals Himself as Father and changes the way in which we perceive Him; He constantly draws us close so that we will understand more about who He is. But eventually, as we mature spiritually, He will instruct us. He shows us His love and then asks us to do something. Some people have the misconception that God's presence makes no demands on us to do things – but often He will show us exactly what we are to do. Yes, those of us only too willing to be given a task rather than resting in His presence, need to learn the art of stillness, but those who love to rest also need to discover that God wants to give them His marching orders. After all, we are in an army!

Jesus had an interesting conversation with a man who understood all about orders: an army captain.[41] Jesus and the captain never actually met, which makes the understanding of obeying orders even more powerful in the story. The Captain has a valued slave who has fallen ill. Hearing of Jesus' power to heal, he sends some elders from the village to plead with Jesus to heal the slave. Jesus agrees to pray for the slave, but on the way to the house the captain sends a message: "Tell Jesus that I am not worthy of Him visiting me. I am not worthy to even meet Him, but being an army man I understand that when a senior officer gives an order then my job is to obey that order without question. I recognise that Jesus has power over sickness, so all He needs to do is give the order and it must happen – my slave will get better." Jesus was gob smacked at the faith of the captain. This man really understood the intrinsic power of authority and command. He had recognised that Jesus was the ranking officer and that His words had huge power – just one word of command was needed. We learn that the slave was indeed healed and Jesus used the captain as an object lesson in faith. The story is also an object lesson in obedience. When the nature, character and motivation of the one giving the commands is pure and good, the orders should be obeyed!

So getting our orders will be a feature of our encounters with God, but what we do with them is up to us. If we obey, then we will learn and grow. If we don't, then we should not be surprised if future encounters consist of God repeating what He has already told us or, heaven forbid, the times of encounter begin to dry up. It is always worth us asking ourselves, "What was the last thing God told me to do?" followed by, "Have I done it yet?" If the answer to this second question is "no", repent and get on with it!

## Bush fire

Let's jump back to Moses for a moment, who we left in chapter 2 making an impassioned plea to God not to leave his people. He was on Mount Sinai – the place where he received the Ten Commandments and also the place where he received his initial orders from God to free His people from the captivity of Egypt. Moses, educated in the top university in the land and related by adoption to the most powerful family in the known world, is out in the wilderness looking after sheep! His previous life of privilege and luxury seems a long time ago. He notices a small tree nearby. There is something strange about it: it appears to be on fire, but the tree still survives. What's going on?

"Moses, stop there," a voice from nowhere says. "Take your shoes off – this is holy sand." Moses knows exactly who is speaking, but is afraid to look. This is a theophany (a God-appearance), with the Angel of the Lord appearing in the guise of a holy fire. God announces Himself to Moses as the God of his forefathers, Abraham, Isaac and Jacob, and calls him to a place of holiness. God reveals something of Moses' destiny and, at this place of encounter, he discovers his calling.

"I've been watching the video footage of my people," God says. "It's horrible hearing their groans, seeing the cruelty they are subjected to. I have come down from Heaven to Earth to rescue them [42] and lead them to the Promised Land – a land of plenty. Your assignment, should you wish to accept it, is to lead them out of Egypt!" (I'm just waiting for God to say this tape will self destruct in five seconds and then the theme music starts!). "Me?" Moses replies. "Who am I? What shall I tell them?" God is quick to reply: "I AM who I am and will be who I will be … tell them I AM has sent you, the God of your ancestors, to bring them here to worship me."

Here God introduces Himself to us as the One who comes down to rescue us. The "Immanuel"[43] nature of God is revealed to Moses. He is also the One who calls us, who speaks to us of our destiny and calling. God tells Moses He wants His people to come and worship Him. The same is true today. The call to worship comes from the place of encounter. Moses would declare, amidst the idols of his day, that the great I AM, the God of his fathers had sent him. In our modern climate of spiritual choice, are we sending out the prophetic call to "Come and worship the one true God"? We too need to take up Moses' mantle and declare amidst our many false gods that "I AM" has sent us.

God defines himself as "I AM". In other words, He is an active *now* being, in the present tense. In the place of encounter we find that God chooses not to be defined by what He has done or is going to do, but by who and what He is right now. Encounter is defined by the immediacy of God. He shows us that His presence is with us, *right now*. He wants Himself to be known as the ever present God, the God of the now. When we encounter God we encounter His present availability. It's pretty amazing that God is looking to meet with you and me, to tell us what His heart is right NOW. Encounter is thrilling. It is the life blood of our faith. It speaks to us, releases us, commissions us. When we encounter God we touch Heaven, sense the will of the Father, and see things we may struggle to rationalise or articulate.

Naturally speaking, Moses was a failed deliverer. He had tried and failed to deliver a Hebrew from the injustice of his Egyptian slave master and ended up murdering the Egyptian. But despite his failed attempt at deliverance, he is not disqualified from being used by God. All he really needs is the knowledge and certainty that God is with him – and this he receives. An encounter with God leaves us different. Moses was equipped with a few special effects to wow the Egyptian court. He practices throwing down his stick which turns into a snake and hiding his hand to reveal it covered with leprosy. As if that is not enough, God tells him to turn the water from the Nile into blood. Moses was not expected to prove God without the support of extraordinary deeds. Miracles should accompany the people of God called for a purpose. Stepping into our destiny should come with the full support of a heavenly arsenal of signs and wonders. To a great extent we have lost the expectation that the supernatural God will support us in our endeavours with supernatural effects. But God backs up His leaders and His people with physical signs of heavenly intervention, otherwise known as spiritual authority. Like Moses, such faith signs are designed to authenticate and guarantee the reliability of the words we bring. The Church needs to expect God to back her up and rely on Him to do so, so that we can demonstrate we are a people worth listening to. Signs prove authority, but they also direct us to the power behind the messenger. Ultimately, miracles point to God.

Recently I was returning to my office after being in a meeting where God had done some great things. I ran across a couple who had been in the meeting also, speaking with a lady who had not. Through chatting to her, I discovered she had a serious back problem. Her spine was being held together with pins and screws, but they were trapping a nerve and as a result she had no feeling in the nerve endings in her legs. We all prayed for her and fairly instantaneously she was surprised that she could feel her toes and move them – something that had not happened for ages. Signs should accompany us when we move in authority. I never discovered this lady's name and don't know where she is from, so I can't offer to authenticate this miracle. All I know is that as I left that woman she was rejoicing that God was for her, loved her, and had not left her out of His amazing plan.

## Feeling weak?

Despite the offer of being backed up by the Almighty, Moses was not totally convinced about his calling and mission. "Look God," he interrupted, "I'm not sure about this whole deal. You see, I'm not all that confident. I'm not an "up front" sort of person. I get all tongue tied when I'm under pressure." God was fairly abrupt in His response: "Shut up! Do what you're told and go!" But Moses was not going to take no for an answer. "Can't you send someone else?" he enquired. What? How can he say that to God. Surely he will be struck by lightning soon! But God says, "You've got a brother, Aaron. He is a good public speaker, he'll do the talking. Now that's enough protesting Moses. You're my man whether you like it or not – now GO!"

The man of faith argues with God. It looks to me like the recipe for a Hebrew BBQ, but somehow Moses has picked up the ancestral argumentative spirit and is prepared to debate the will of God with the Maker Himself! Did you realise you have a God you can argue with? He is not offended when we disagree with Him, since He is not sitting in Heaven just waiting for us to step out of line so He can beat us with a stick. I enjoy it when my kids express their own opinions about things, even if they are wrong, and so does God. What kind of father would want kids who did everything they were told, but never thought for themselves or experienced real life? Similarly, God desires to protect, guide and nurture us, but not control us.

There is great news for us all in the Moses story. We may feel tongue tied and useless, but God can demonstrate Himself through our inadequacy or lack of skill. He chooses to outwork His plans through us, rather than bypassing us. The weakness of Moses did not deter the call of God – weakness does not disqualify us from achieving our destiny! As the story unfolds we see that God's presence goes with Moses and his people. Neither the stuttering of Moses or the eloquence of Aaron can change the fact that God is with them. God could have chosen some classy performer to be His spokesperson before Pharaoh, but He didn't. He chose Moses. If God is on your case, know that He will take responsibility for both the message and the messenger.

## The role of weakness

Weakness seems to be a requirement for God using us. Paul the apostle describes humanity as fragile clay jars containing treasure.[44] He goes on to lament the existence of an unnamed "thorn in his flesh" (possibly some ongoing debilitating illness) and recounts a conversation with God where *"… three times I begged the Lord to take it away. Each time he said, 'My grace is all you need. My power works best in weakness.'"*[45] In Paul's God encounter he was being taught that God's power works best through someone who is weak. If you are strong in body and mind then you may find this news a bit alarming. Being strong is something that humans have always prized, from the Greek Olympic arena to the Oxford spires. Strength is something we desire above all things. But let's focus again on that pearl necklace. How much do we desire the things of God – His presence and power, the evidence of His Kingdom – to be expressed through us? Being a Pearl Hunter demands everything, EVERYTHING!

Our strength, our intellect, our charismatic personality are all to be laid on the altar. Paul manages to articulate the effect of embracing weakness in the pursuit of the presence:

*"So now I am glad to boast about my weakness, so that the power of Christ can work through me. That's why I take pleasure in my weakness, and in the insults, hardships, persecutions, and troubles that I suffer for Christ. For when I am weak, then I am strong."* [46]

Good news for strong people everywhere: you can be strong as you find power in weakness. The power you really need is not a striving, pushy power, but a silent, unseen power that comes directly from Heaven. Whatever our natural strengths are, we will find out how God can use them as we surrender in obedience to Him. Our character and being can be infused with the power of God, but we will have to die first. If we are to be carriers of the presence, to display God's glory, to go on a Holy Spirit adventure, then we must yield and allow weakness to become our strength.

I have always been a leader, always wanted to do stuff, always wanted to make a difference. But after the first three years of leading our local church I had come to the end of whatever I had naturally. I had been in business for fifteen years and to begin with I applied just about everything I'd ever learned – with mixed consequences. We ended up better, more stable, and with a clearer sense of direction than ever before, but I wasn't sure we had what we needed to get us through the next leg of the journey. In hindsight, I can see a four-year process of me dying to my leadership gifting, of me coming to the place where I realised I didn't have what it would take to do the job God was calling us to do. Climbing on the altar and dying has been painful. As a dear friend says, "The trouble with living sacrifices is that they have a habit of climbing off the altar." The urge to give up, go back into business and do something which would make me feel useful again had been surging through my soul for all of those four years, but I knew I could not escape the call of destiny that came every time I encountered God. I was just going to have to die to go on! Have I died? I'm not totally sure. Some days I feel as if I have nothing to prove and during those times I feel that I lead well and people respond. Other days I am so anxious to do something and prove something that I feel the art of being a good leader slipping away from me. I suppose I have some more dying to do!

## Becoming the servant

In the pantomime *Cinderella*, Prince Charming changes places with his servant Dandini, (oh no he didn't ... oh yes he did!). The Prince takes a lower place in order to achieve something he couldn't do as a prince. There is another story of a Prince, the Prince of Heaven who took on the very nature of a servant in order to secure the permanent and lasting presence of God for us. This Prince came from His home, not to do what He wanted, but to do what His Father commissioned Him to do.[47] He was still fully God – God was pleased to fully and completely live inside of Him,[48] rightly calling him Emmanuel: God with us,[49] but Christ emptied Himself of all His divine power. His divine privileges were halted at the moment of incarnation as He stepped out of the palace courts of Heaven. Literally, He "neutralised" Himself, surrendering His equality and His "rights" to obedience.[50] He had no privileges, no dignity. He was fully human.

The notion of "God with us" allows us access to His presence and takes the encounter to a new level. We no longer have a distant God, separated by anger or sin, but rather an intensely personal God – One who takes His long term relationship with humanity very seriously. This idea of God with us continues at

Pentecost when God pours out His Holy Spirit.[51] Jesus has made it possible for a divine encounter to happen for young or old, male or female, in fact anyone who wants it.[52] Pentecost makes the potential to experience the presence of God possible. Visitation is no longer reserved for special people and special times. The way is blown wide open for divine encounters all the time. The Holy Spirit comes time and time again, when you ask Him to come. Encounters come to all who cry out to Him. The starting place is obedience and surrender.

## Endnotes

38. John 14:31
39. Matthew 7:21
40. 1 John 5:3
41. Luke 7:1-10
42. Exodus 3:8
43. Meaning "God with us"
44. 2 Corinthians 4:7
45. 2 Corinthians 12:8
46. 2 Corinthians 12:9-10
47. John 6:38
48. Colossians 1:19; 2:9
49. Matthew 1:23
50. Philippians 2:5-7
51. Acts 2
52. Acts 2:17-18

# Promises

Woven into the design of our world is the intension of our Designer. It is no accident that man rules the earth, has huge ingenuity, continually has new ideas and continually reproduces himself all over the face of the world. It is supposed to be like that. The invisible thread of the created tapestry is the word that was spoken over creation when it was in the process of being created. Before humanity's first day on earth there was nothing at all. At the beginning of day one God spoke the words "Light, be" and the lights were turned on. I dare say that one day we will all be able to watch the equivalent of a divine DVD of creation and see exactly how it was done. Better still, maybe we could view the experience in real time, since Heaven sits outside of the human time continuum.

God's string of verbal commands continued until day six, the day man was created. All of creation was in place, now all that was needed was someone to rule over it. So God formed the very image of Himself, *"… to be like ourselves"*[53]. Man was made in God's image. The hunger we have for spiritual things, our desire for the divine, our need to relate to God – all of these things were hardwired into our system at creation. We are spiritual beings created to function just like God. This explains why, in addition to man's creativity and ingenuity, religion is such a potent force all over our planet. The spiritual aspect of man's nature can't just be explained away. We are designed to be captured by the divine, enticed by the thought of God. It's hardly surprising that Karl Marx described the alluring effects of religion as the "opiate of the people". Similarly, the early believers were accused of being out of control drunks at Pentecost! [54]

## God and Man – artists creating

Since man is meant to reflect the very image and essence of God, it is no wonder that we long to create. God created us to be creative and every human has the desire to create! At the most fundamental level, we create other human beings, and normally have a lot of fun in the creation process. What could be more creative than that? I believe that God also had a lot of fun creating the earth. When we read the account of Creation in Genesis, it is very tempting to tap into the sombre mood of the big screen biblical epics of year's ago – imagining a Charlton Hestonesque God with a long white beard and a deep voice. But whenever I read those words, I see instead an artist at work having an immense amount of fun. I'm married to an artist and when she is in her studio doing her work, she is at her happiest. I come in to say hi and her face is shining because she is spending time creating, playing, turning a thought into something. That is the scene here in Genesis. God is having fun, He is excited, He is in mid-process: "I can't stop now, I've just had an amazing idea for a red fruit or is it a vegetable?" He creates something and says, "That will keep them guessing!" as He brings into being what is later called a tomato (He leaves the naming process to us). Just like God, man's creative urge is very strong. We are made to make stuff, to express ourselves, to make a mark on our world. Creativity is expressed in the entrepreneur's latest business idea, the engineer's plans, the administrator's new process. If man is anywhere he will create things, make things happen.

What relevance does this have to pursuing the presence of God? God's presence is the catalyst that sparks our creativity like nothing else. His presence is not intended just to give us goose bumps in a highly charged worship meeting. Where God is, there is creativity – it flows out of His very being; it is an integral part of His character. Not surprisingly then, when the tangible presence of God is around, it causes our creative urges to come to the fore. There is something about proximity to the divine nature that switches on all our creative lights. And the nearer to Him we get, the more creative we become.

Throughout the history of the Church there has been a strong connection between artistic expression and our spiritual journey (apart from the Puritan season of Church history which tried to remove the clutter from faith and bring the Word of God to pre-eminence). We see it in the beauty of architecture, the expressive altar cloths in cathedrals, and the recent rise in artists painting during our worship services. Aside from these, music represents the most obvious creative expression. There is something about music that connects man to God. I find very little mention of music in the early part of Scripture, but when we get to the Tabernacle of David, we see that he ordered continual worship and praise to God with accompanying music. Most of the psalms are the lyrics of songs that were sung to the Lord in the tabernacle.

If, as Scripture says, we are supposed to be "fruitful and multiply" – i.e. to continue to populate the earth and express our creativity in other ways – then the more we appreciate, pursue and encounter the presence of God, the more we will fulfil this mandate. An increase in the presence of God in our lives will bring a proportional increase in fruitfulness. Fruit is the sign that all is well with the tree – the apple tree produces apples. Fruit comes when the tree is planted in the right place and is subject to the right conditions. God has planted our lives with the intention of them being fruitful in every aspect – our money, our relationships, our work, our emotions. If we want to be fruitful, we need to embrace God's presence more and more. The closer we get to Him, the more we will "multiply" in every area.

*Relationship* is another underlying theme in the creation of mankind. The "us" of God is relational. In the creation of mankind we see all three Persons of the Trinity involved. God is a highly relational being and has therefore created us to be too. Not only does this mean that humans need to have a relationship with God, but they must have relationships with each other. No matter how introverted you are, you have been created as a relational being. You need other people and you need God. There can be no peace, no feeling of wholeness for a person unless both of these needs are fulfilled: a healthy relationship with God and healthy relationships with others. In our individualistic society we have to guard against the enemy's device of isolation. All of us need some space, some time alone, and this has merit especially when we use that time to seek God. But it is never meant to be a permanent state. We have an individual, personal relationship with God, but very often He deals with His people corporately, as we all as individually. We find His individual attention and yet He also speaks to us in community. Nowhere is this more true than in His communication to the Body of Christ. He loves us individually, but loves us as a community and cherishes our "togetherness".

Having a wife and four daughters has helped me enormously to get my head around this. Do I love each of them fully? Yes, of course. Do I love each of them differently? Yes, they are all individuals. Is there something about the family that I love? Yes, that is how I relate to them all, as the father of my family.

We have a bond as a group, a love that is not just individual, but shared together. In addition, I now have a son in law and that love is expanded to include him as part of the group, and he is loved by us all. God creates us as unique individuals, but "individualism" as the world sees it, is a deception. That is why we as the Church must guard against the erosion of our gatherings. The writer of Hebrews urged the saints not to give up meeting together [55], in the context of encouraging one another to enter boldly into the presence of God. When we come together we are expressing something of the corporate nature of God's relationship with us.

The third dynamic of the nature of God seen in Genesis and imparted to us is "ruling." Being the boss is also a part of the human reflection of the nature and image of God. If you believe in God then you probably don't have much problem with the idea of him being the Big Boss, but this is also a function that He gave to mankind. We reflect his rulership. We are all, in a way, supposed to rule – to rule over our surroundings, rule over our emotions, rule in whatever sphere of life we have been given responsibility. Different people are given different measures of responsibility, according to their capacity, but the basic truth is the same: we should "reign over..." or "rule" all areas of our life.

One of the strategies the enemy uses to undermine this God-given function is to get us out of control. It's a simple equation: if we are out of control of an aspect of our life, then we are not ruling over it as God intended. We can see the devastation that is caused by someone who has an addiction – it incapacitates them and prevents them from making decisions. It removes their free will and causes them to be subject to another force. Addiction is a demonic strategy that grips too many people in today's society. It is a perversion of rule, enslaving the individual so that the ruler becomes the demon!

What about our emotions? Many people allow their emotions to rule and therefore run their lives. Our emotions are powerful internal forces that are there for a reason. But that reason is so that we can enjoy and experience life on a multi-sensory level. They give colour to life, but were never intended to become forces that govern us. Instead we are to govern them! When we don't "feel" like going to work, what are we going to do? Give into that emotion or get up and go to work despite our feelings? Some people are more feeling-orientated than others, so this is more of a problem for some and less so for others, but nevertheless, we cannot allow our feelings to control us. If we do then we will lose control. The converse can also be true for those who are more clinical and analytical. If we allow ourselves to be controlled by Spock-like logic, then we are going to have a fairly dull existence! The answer is to be led by the Holy Spirit in all we do. The person who is surrendered to the Spirit has the divine presence of God at work within them to govern their will, emotions and thoughts.

Whether you are a government minister, a computer programmer, a student, a homemaker, unemployed, retired, or anything else, you were made to rule your surroundings. The decisions you make that affect your day's outcome are all in your power to rule. The kids don't have to get you down every day, your husband doesn't have to irritate you, your work doesn't have to be tedious – as a ruler you are called to govern the sphere you have been given. It is part of the nature of God in you, part of the design. You don't have to become a bossy boots all of a sudden, but start by grabbing hold of the principle that you are designed to rule. Start to imagine yourself the way God intends you to be, and then let Him work in you and lead you.

As we pursue and enjoy the presence of God, something wonderful will happen in each of these areas: our creative abilities, our relationships and our ability to rule and reign in life. The presence blesses each one of them and we begin to be more innovative; our relationships become more meaningful; we find ourselves in greater control of our lives (even as we learn to surrender more!). The presence fulfils us and makes us whole. We begin to live more like we are supposed to live.

## Moses returns to the place of encounter

It was now two months to the day since Pharaoh capitulated and allowed the mass of Hebrews to leave the captivity of Egypt. It took all the sign-working gifts that Moses had been given to do the job, and it was possible only after a complete massacre of Egypt's children during which the king's heir to the throne was struck down. Only after this severe blow did Pharaoh actually release Moses to lead the Hebrews out.

Incidentally, if it took such signs and wonders to assist Moses in his quest, if it took Jesus signs and wonders to get people to believe in His divinity and message, why do we think it will take anything less to get people's attention today?

I heard of a Chinese pastor who was commenting on the state of the Western Church. Someone asked him why people were not getting saved in large numbers in the West. He replied simply that it was due to the lack of power in the Western Church! Paul rebuked the Galatian church: *"You are following a different way that pretends to be the Good News but is not the Good News at all."*[56] In short, a gospel of words is not the Gospel at all. Moses needed the power of God to release the captives. Jesus needed the power of God to announce and release the Kingdom of God. The apostolic fathers needed the power of God to found the Church and proclaim the Good News. How much more then do we need it? And that power is birthed only in the place of encounter – the place of presence. In His presence, the same Holy Spirit that resulted in the disciples power and boldness, is poured out on us.

Now Moses returns to the desert of Sinai – the place where he had his burning bush experience. How things have changed. Instead of being a shepherd of sheep, Moses is now shepherding the people of God. Then God appears to him and shocks us with these words:

*"Now if you will obey me and keep my covenant, you will be my own special treasure from among all the peoples on earth; for all the earth belongs to me. And you will be my kingdom of priests, my holy nation."*[57]

Let's just pick this over a little because it holds so much about the intent and heart of God. A superficial reading of Scripture makes an artificial distinction between the God of the Old Testament (judgement, anger, law) and the God of the New Testament (love, grace, mercy), which has caused many to almost throw away the pearl of great price as they discard the old for the sake of the new. But this is founded on a misunderstanding of God's original intent.

## Covenant

We have already seen that in Genesis there is a covenant or promise innate to all humanity. God decrees that we are to fill the earth, multiply, and rule over it. These are essentially one-sided covenants. God promises this will happen, regardless of our actions and behaviour. He does not require us to do anything[58], and this is why man prospers, multiplies, is creative, brings rule over the planet (even if he is very unwise with his governance of the earth's resources) while sin and godlessness rule. These are the effects of the one-sided covenant that does not require us to do anything except live! Because Adam and Eve disobeyed God and ate from the banned tree, they missed out on Eden and all its benefits, but this did not negate God's essential covenant promise – we just live out that promise in a substantially poorer way than God intended and with very different results.

The next covenant God makes is with Noah, the rainbow being the sign of that promise[59]. The decay and sin on the earth was grieving God so much that He first of all decided to shorten the life span of the average human to 120 years maximum. One of the causes of His grief was the "sons of god" (referring to a group of fallen angels)[60] somehow taking human form [61] and seeking to marry human women. Who knows what genetic chaos would have ensued. Added to that, humans on their own seemed totally orientated towards evil and the Bible relates that they would only imagine evil all the time. Darkness was everywhere and the world was growing darker. This literally *"broke* [God's] *heart"* and caused Him to come to the decision to "re-set" the Earth and re-establish His covenant with man. Thankfully, one man and his family remained righteous so they were instructed to build the ark.

Something must have gone very wrong with the world in order for God to start again. It wasn't the fundamental design that was wrong, but a mixture of sinful decay and the decision of a few former angels to deliberately mess with the Designer's boundaries for existence. The Earth had become like a PC, painfully grinding along, getting slower and slower because of all the downloads and poorly designed software installations. But now it has caught an unsolvable virus too, a deliberate attempt to sabotage its function once and for all. In such a situation there are few options. If this happens to us, we can either throw the thing across the room in frustration and begin again with a Mac (this is what I did), or you can wipe the hard drive and reset it, begin again from scratch. God chose to press the reset button.

God "wiped" the earth with a huge flood (I believe this, but we don't need to get too hung up on the logistics). He repopulated it with animals and, of course, its first new family. The creation covenant was reiterated. God expressed the first sign that mankind would need laws to govern them (saying, don't kill other people). Then He made a promise never to reset the Earth in this way ever again, confirming His promise with a rainbow. The rainbow was the sign of God's unconditional covenant for the future of humanity; the sign of the intrinsic promise that God is over the earth, the earth is His – that one day He will come back for all those who trust in Him and set things in their proper order.

Next up on the promise front is Abraham. The filling and multiplication mandate is taken a bit further. Abraham is made a covenant to become *"… a great nation"* and *"… blessed."*[62] God is after a special, chosen people. He wants relationship. He wants to be with men. He wants His presence to be felt. This helps us understand and "feel" the heartbeat of God – He desires to relate to mankind; He wants to be in relationship with us. So God makes an *"everlasting covenant"*[63]– one that is still in force today, and those who live by faith are the inheritors of this promise[64], as well as something of this promise being left for the current Jews. The condition of the Abrahamic covenant was circumcision – ouch! – as a sign of devotion (talk to any man and he will tell you that it *has* to be an act of devotion to go through with it). The equivalent for the modern believer is baptism.

## Mosaic covenant

Moses is standing in the presence of God on the Mount of Encounter and God speaks this incredible promise requiring obedience:

*"Now if you will obey me and keep my covenant, you will be my own special treasure from among all the peoples on earth; for*

*all the earth belongs to me. And you will be my kingdom of priests,*
*my holy nation"* [65]

The covenant bit gets most of the attention in the rest of the
torah. The Ten Commandments form the basis of law for the
Hebrews and have become the basis of most of the world's legal
systems. Moses then has several conversations with God after
the Commandments are given which go into more detail about
how a community should live, what are their social responsibil-
ities, and what standards are needed to maintain God's presence
among His people. Throughout the books following on from
Genesis references are constantly made regarding the obligations
of the people of God and their need to keep the Law, which of
course they were completely unable to do, pointing towards
Christ and His ability to keep the Law and fulfil all of its
requirements.

But what of the actual promise of God? It is the promise
that goes to the heart of God, His intention, the consequence
of His presence being with us.

## "Special treasure"

My wife is brilliant at feeding our girls with self esteem and
value. Often I will find her with one of our kids snuggled up
on her lap where she is whispering value and worth into their
ears. They wriggle, giggle, get shy, tell her to stop being silly,
but something truly wonderful is happening during these
moments. She is affirming them as totally loved; she is expressing
confidence in them; she is helping them to feel at home. When
I do the same I am helping shape their identities and direction
for their lives. God Himself modelled this for us, expressing
His love and commitment to His beloved people, telling us
how much we are valued and wanted. Father God lavishes
undeserved praise on our heads, feeds us with His affection
and attention. Remember, this is the same God who once

wiped the planet clean, who knew all the wrong stuff people
would continue to do in the future. But He expresses His love
and commitment for His people to Moses, and He continues
to do so to us today. Have our own kids done stuff wrong? Of
course! Will our kids do stuff that is wrong again? Of course!
Does that change the way we feel about them? Of course not!
DO YOU GET IT? Here, at the very point of spelling out the
harshness of the Law, here at the moment when the Law
covenant is being established, the true heartbeat of God is
revealed – that of a great Father who speaks to us as His *special
treasure*.

I have spoken of our relationship with God, the pursuit of
His presence as the pearl of great price, something of infinite
worth. Here is God telling us that our affection and devotion is
His pearl of great price. Our relationship with Him is worth
more than He can value. It is worth Him sacrificing everything
to get our affection, our love! Yes, worth sacrificing *everything*.
Does the sacrifice of His Son make sense now? When you are
totally passionate about something, it is worth spending everything to have it. That was what God's sacrifice of his own Son
was all about. It was not the action of some divine "child
abuser"; not the action of Someone who *needed* our affirmation.
But, rather the action of a passionate Lover prepared to do anything for His bride!

## "Kingdom of priests"

The Hebrew nation was not yet in existence. Instead they were
an asylum-seeking people group on the move, waiting for
resettlement after escaping oppression. Yet, God sees and refers
to them as a kingdom. He calls them a "kingdom of priests".
At this stage the priesthood had not yet been formalised, but
we learn later that priests will be go-betweens, standing before
God representing man.

Today we need to rise to our calling to be a "kingdom of priests" – a nation of devoted followers who have access to God's presence and are able to stand before His awesome power. We need to know both the tender whisper of a loving parent in our ear and the awesome splendour and power of the King to establish His Kingdom. We are both a "special treasure" and part of a "kingdom of priests" – the former speaking of God's special affection for us and the latter of His power and authority invested in us as we act on His behalf.

I have found in my walk with God that there are times when He is my Father and times when he is my King. There are times when I pour out my complaints, my heart, my sob stories to Him and the gentle, loving hand of the Father is there to caress and comfort me. These are wonderful, precious times in the embrace of the Father. There are other times when I am standing in the court of the King of kings, where the tender embrace is not appropriate, where something lofty, awesome, something of majesty is happening. In the seasons of our church life we need to be aware of the moment. Is it time to minister to God as priests or time to embrace Him as Daddy? There is a time and place to express both. Will the King kill you if you refer to him as Daddy when you should be calling Him King? Of course not, but let's grow up in our faith. Can you imagine Prince Charles shouting across Westminster Abbey during some official engagement, "Mummy, I want a cuddle!" Err, no! Likewise, can you imagine Charles saying to her, after she has completed a long, exhausting day of appointments, "Your Majesty, would you like a cup of tea?" One occasion calls for formality but the other invites familiarity. In the same way the Church needs to grow up and move on from immature concepts. Yes, we need to embrace a childlike relationship with our Father, but we also need to understand the majesty of the King.

The kingdom of priests that God referred to saw its partial fulfilment in the reign of David, but speaks more fully of the Kingdom Jesus came to inaugurate. We were always intended to be part of the kingdom of priests who would fill the earth and rule over it. Our lives are supposed to be empowered to stand before God and bring about the fullness of His Kingdom, the place where God resides. The current strategy of the Church has to be to raise up powerful priests to take the authority of God to the ends of the earth, working from a place of treasured affection.

## "Holy Nation"

The final part of God's expression of His heart to Moses was to call His people a "holy nation". In other words, a people "set aside" to honour God. The community of God's people is supposed to be holy, dedicated, devoted, sanctified. Holiness is the very nature of God. He Himself is sacred, set apart, unable to be defiled by sin. He desires the same for us. God wishes not only to lavish His affection on us, not only to be our King, but that we become a holy community, a people whose devotion sets them apart to God.

This brings us back to the point of the very first chapter. What differentiates the people of God from everyone else? The people of God are supposed to be holy. We are supposed to be different! "Holiness" sometimes gets a bad press because we so frequently try to aspire to it through sheer effort. In actual fact, we are supposed to display the holiness of God by spending an increasing amount of time in His presence. We are to reflect His holiness, not try to create our own. When we try to be holy through our own effort, we try to live under the Law once more instead of by grace, and all that happens is we become critical, judgmental and feel guilty. This is the burden of religion as opposed to relationship. No, time in the presence of God is the best way to be holy.

*"You are a chosen people. You are royal priests, a holy nation, God's very own possession"* [66] is Peter the apostle's way of expressing this covenant. God speaks to Moses about His intention while Peter addresses the Church and tells them who they ACTUALLY ARE! God's desire expressed at Sinai is now a reality in the Church. Moses may have experienced the burning bush, but you inherit the promise of the encounter.

## Endnotes

53. Genesis 1:26-28
54. Acts 2:13-15
55. Hebrews 10:25
56. Galatians 1:6-7
57. Exodus 19:5-6
58. I recognise that this is not an explicit covenant, God does not use that word specifically, but it is implied and is widely seen at the first covenant.
59. Genesis 9:12-13
60. In the Old Testament the expression "sons of god" was used only of angels, (Job 1:6; 2:1; 38:7)
61. References to the group of angels that were cast out are 2 Peter 2:4 and Jude 1:6
62. Genesis 12:2-3
63. Genesis 17:7
64. Galatians 3:6-9
65. Exodus 19:5-6
66. 1 Peter 2:9

# CHAPTER 6

# Fear, Frustration and Fatigue

Can someone tell my why the feelings of wanting to "give up" are regular and cyclical? I am sure it has a lot to do with my personality, although I am not given to bouts of depression. Life for me is pretty up and down, rather than level and easy. I feel a bit like the granny in the movie *Cheaper by the Dozen*. She tells a story of how she used to visit the fairground when she was a child. Some kids liked to go on the merry-go-round while others – like her – would always go on the rollercoaster. But, she says, it always made her feel sick. When asked why she didn't go on the merry-go-round instead so that she wouldn't feel sick, she replies, "Where would be the fun in that?!" Experiencing life with all its uncertainty, energy and trouble is much more exciting than living an untroubled but flat existence. I am pretty sure that we believers are supposed to feel the up and down nature of life too. Life for us is no merry-go-round, even though we try our hardest to smooth out the bumps!

I am not sure why we try to make life easy for ourselves. Do we really want a sun bed lifestyle all the time? If you stay on a sun bed too long you'll get burnt! Whoever promised us an easy life anyway? The preacher who said, "Come to Jesus and all your worries will disappear" was wrong! Anyone who has been a believer for any period of time will tell you there is nothing easy about being one.

The "easy life" is a dream that doesn't exist in reality. The X-Factor teaches us that fame and riches are possible for that "special one" and encourages all the hopefuls to think that the "one" might be them. The pages of Hello magazine hammer home the dream of a celebrity lifestyle we all ought to aspire to. But none of these dreams ultimately deliver that which they promise. For all who "make it" the press is littered with twice as many casualties – one hit wonders whose careers have gone down the pan, tales of alcohol addiction, sex scandals and every other kind of scandal that rips the hearts out of the celebrity B-list. There is a spirit behind these things, of course. A spirit that spins a lie that Heaven is Porsche-Rolex-D&G lifestyle and sets out its false expectations of how to achieve it. Once we get locked into the dream of a better life, fed by a stream of material needs, money inevitably becomes the all-consuming objective; a good income and a good return on investments becomes our safety net to a better future.

I am writing this at the tail end of one of the worst economic meltdowns in recent history. Pension plans were decimated, investments halved, jobs lost. The problems can be traced back to greed and the fuelling of the material dream using money we didn't have. Whether it was the bank's greed by making hay while the sun was shining or my greed in wanting the next overpriced luxury, it was greed all the same. My observation has been that all this greed – and particularly the thought that, through recession, it might be suddenly curtailed – has led to one thing: *fear*. Fear has been stirred up and perpetuated by the media. The press has sensationalized every twist and turn of the economic downturn with front page headlines. TV news channels have prophesied disaster on every bulletin. One news channel even displayed a graphic showing a downward pointing arrow with the word RECESSION emblazoned underneath for months to reinforce the dire state of the nation. I don't want to take away from the reality of the trauma many businesses and individuals have suffered, but all of this speaks of more than just the facts. Paul the apostle wrote, "Set your thoughts on things above"[67] but we have done the opposite, becoming prophets of doom. How much of this pervasive attitude has rubbed off on the Church I wonder? To what extent have we allowed the spirit of the age to capture our thinking? Has not the spirit of fear behind all that is going on won a victory and quenched the faith of believers?

## Toxic fear

Fear is a killer. It will rob you of joy; it will rob you of peace; it will rob you of freedom. Fear interrupts our lives constantly: we fear losing our stuff so we buy more insurance than we need. We fear dying of some disease so we eat organic food, exercise at overpriced gyms and pop vitamin supplements. There is a swine flu epidemic so we walk about with medical face masks. We hear that coffee is going to be in short supply so we panic buy at the supermarket. We fear for our children's safety so we overprotect them. The list goes on. It is an age-old trick of the enemy: cultivate a need in people then take it away from them – bingo, fear!

Fear however is toxic to the presence of God. Faith – the antithesis of fear – is the means by which we encounter God. We are saved by faith and we are called to live by faith. Without faith we cannot see God [68]. Faith is pretty important if we are to experience the abiding presence of God in our lives. Put fear amongst a group of believers and it will dissipate the presence of God faster than you can believe it. I was once in a meeting where the Spirit of God was moving upon people wonderfully and suddenly a man who was ill collapsed. A prophet friend of mine who was with me in the meeting said he actually saw the spirit of death walk into the room and hit this man. Well fear just gripped the meeting, not tangibly, but that was pretty much it for the day in terms of any sense of the Spirit of God being able to move. We are supposed to be alert to the devices the enemy deploys to catch us off guard, so how come we're so vulnerable to fear? It's his number one strategy. If the devil can hit us with an unexpected bill, a sudden sickness, or sow doubt in your mind, he will. But we have to choose what to do with that fear. We can either let it rob us or we can counteract it with something else. The Bible teaches us that, *"Perfect love expels all fear"*[69] so trusting in God is clearly the ultimate answer. But at times that can be easier said than done.

When there was a wonderful move of the Holy Spirit in renewal all over the world in the 1990's one of the "problems" most people had with it was rooted in fear – a fear of the unknown. Some of the strange manifestations that occurred as the Holy Spirit moved worried people – their main concern being a fear of being deceived by a counterfeit experience manufactured by the enemy. In fact, the history of the Charismatic movement is replete with such fears. It has been a well-used tool to prevent people from embracing the move of the Spirit. Fear manifests itself as people express their wariness of that which they do not understand, as preachers urge caution or even speak against the move, as theologians try to suggest that such manifestations are unbiblical. The consequence of all this fear, well-intentioned or not, is to quench the presence of God.

Pioneering leaders such as John and Carol Arnott, who were used to release a wave of the power of the Spirit as they hosted the outbreak of the Toronto blessing in their church, have had to get used to coming against such fear in public meetings. They realized they needed to create a platform of faith over which the Spirit of God could ride into town! It is one reason why "revival meetings" take so long (the other is that some preachers like the sound of their own voices and don't know when to stop!) If fear (or its cousin doubt) is in the room, then it is going to take faith to counteract it. Faith comes when we start to hear the Word of God and, in a revival meeting setting, when it is backed up with some sign that points to the Logos, Jesus –something to make the doubter wonder whether, actually, this could be authentic.

What stops the presence from settling amid your life? It is more than likely fear – fear of letting go, fear of letting God because of what the Holy Spirit might discover and, as a result, what you will have to deal with. Fear is just hanging around looking to get in at a moment's notice. It lurks around us waiting for an opening. We will not experience the fullness of God's presence if fear has captured our heart. Instead we need to allow the love of God to expel the fear so that we can enter and abide in His presence.

## Can you hear the blast of the horn?

We return to Moses. He comes down from the mountain where God has just spoken over him His promised affection and purposes for the people of God[70]. Moses tells the elders and all the people that God has told him and they respond by telling Moses they will do whatever God has said. Good start! This could be good for the people of God – they may actually fulfil the promises of God. Whoopee!

Then Moses goes back up the mountain and God speaks of coming upon the people in a thick cloud. The cloud is the presence of God and it will operate something like a PA system: the people will be able to hear God wherever the cloud goes (great technology – could be the answer to people constantly moaning the church PA is too loud or too quiet!) Along with this revelation, God gives Moses some very precise instructions about encountering His presence. First, the people should be consecrated by washing their clothes. Cleansing will be a characteristic part of entering the presence of God. Then the people are told to be ready and to expect the arrival of the cloud on the third day (the "third day" in Scripture carries powerful significance – Jesus rose from the dead on the third day). Third, they are to set a boundary line which neither people nor animals can cross – the presence is a holy place! Finally, only when there comes a blast of the horn *"the people may go up on the mountain"* and encounter and experience the presence of God.

As New Covenant believers we have freedom to access the presence of God at any time, but there are some principles (rather than rules) to learn from Moses that show us what will help or hinder us from experiencing the presence of God. First, we see that "washing" ourselves is important. We need to be mindful of confessing to the Lord any sins that have got in the way of our relationship with Him. The sin problem has been permanently dealt with forever through Christ, but sin is still a present problem to the believer. The New Testament practice of baptism has a washing effect; it is the power sign that our sins are washed away. But we still need to confess our sins to God regularly as the reality of our salvation is experienced on a daily basis.

Second, we need to be expectant. God promised His presence to the people and they fully expected Him to come; expected nothing less than to see and hear Him, in fact. Why would we expect anything less? One of the struggles God's people face today is that we don't live expectant of hearing His voice and experiencing His presence on an ongoing basis. Scepticism (another relative of fear) has a habit of blocking our expectancy and we allow it to remain, rock solid, and adopt a "God will have to hit me to get my attention" type of attitude. I have seen enough to know that God will hit you if He needs to – if that's what it will take for you to not be sceptical any more. I have seen God come in such power on a sceptic that they fall over! It tends to knock the scepticism out of them quite quickly! Our expectancy is important to receiving God. The more we hunger and thirst for Him the more likely we are to receive and experience Him.

Boundary lines are the next agenda item. The people of God were given a clear line they were not to cross. But the boundaries lines have been moved for us. There is nothing to prevent us from approaching and entering the presence of God, but there are times when our approach to the Lord needs to be different. I talked in the previous chapter about coming before him as a child or as a king. There are times when, at the boundary of His presence, we need to check ourselves before Him. Boundaries give us an opportunity to reflect, to consider what God is doing at this time, to check our heart and motives. We are not going to be stoned to death for crossing a line, but I suggest that careful reflection would be good.

Finally, in our analogy, we are told that at the sound of the horn we can ascend into God's presence. It denotes a special time when we are given the "all clear" to enter His presence. We need to understand that we are living in a wonderful season of the horn blast. The horn is sounding as I write. The time is ripe to experience the fullness of the presence, so come on up!

Moses comes back down the mountain and makes all the preparations ready for this amazing encounter. The people are going to experience the presence of God in a powerful way. This is the sort of meeting to arrive early for! The third day arrives, Moses and Aaron go on up and they are given the executive summary. God delivers the Big 10 to them. They are ten revolutionary truths – we decided to call them laws –

which are actually instructions that will lead the people to
know God and His nature more fully. Then the horn sounds
and it is time for all the people to go up the mountain. An awesome spectacle ensues. The cloud whirls around and thunders
with the sound of God's voice. Lightning flashes through the
cloud. It is too much for those who witness it from afar. The
people are literally shaken to the core. They are so afraid that
they implore Moses to go up the mountain without them. In
other words, they opt for a "third party" experience of the
presence, rather than experiencing it first hand. Fear robbed
them of the presence. Moses calls to the people, "Don't be
afraid, for God has come in this way to test you, and so that
your fear of Him will keep you from sinning!"[71] but, fear had
so gripped their hearts that they stayed at a safe distance.

This is a salutary lesson in what the fear of God can do. Not
the kind of holy fear that Moses is alluding to, the kind that
stops us from sinning, the kind of fear which is an awesome
respect for God's holiness. Rather this is a debilitating fear, a
"Wait till your father gets home" kind of fear. It is a fear
founded not on an experience of the love of God, but a false
assumption that He is angry and distant. Moses had already
faced and overcome the latter kind of fear. His experience of
God was such that, though this moment was awesome and
frightening, an excitement and anticipation propelled him
forward instead of holding him back. The people, on the other
hand, did not know God in the same way.

Last year I took the kids to Disneyland. The Space Mountain
rollercoaster has a great rocket launcher that propels you into
darkness. There is a boom, the rocket is launched, and people
scream as they plunge into darkness. My eldest girls were
apprehensive and a little fearful about the experience, but they
went for it; they were brave enough. My youngest daughter
was glued to me, however, and refused to go on. Fear had rooted

her to the spot and stopped her from having the experience. Fear resulted in excitement for the others, but became a barrier to one (though it gave me a good excuse to keep my feet on the ground). This is what we are talking about – fear that either paralyses us from entering the presence of God or fear that brings us to an exciting experience of Him! Which will we choose?

## The face of God

As I write this chapter I am on holiday in Spain. We are in a villa and my youngest daughter came out and asked my wife how to work the DVD player. I laughed, of course, because the idea of my wife troubleshooting a technology problem is, well laughable! I got up and sorted the problem. I came back to the veranda where we are sitting and said, "I can't imagine why she asked you to sort the DVD out." Deborah replied, "It's because you have your serious face on because you're concentrating and she is scared of you!" This is the girl that at other times will run up to me and fling her arms round me and say, "I love you." The face of God can sometimes look scary. Most of the time, however, it is the loving face of a Father. Moses would regularly meet with God face to face in the tent of meeting. The cloud would fall on it and Moses would talk to the Father just like a friend. But to the people watching from a distance, this was a scary moment, God meeting with a Man! How well do you know your Father? There are times when His face is scary, but His eyes are still the loving eyes of a Father. God the Father is not always a kiss and cuddle Father – at times He is very serious and always holy, awesome and powerful – but He is still always your Father and you His child. He is still your Dad in Heaven and willing to cuddle you – same Dad, just a different face! Maturity teaches us to engage with Father God in different ways but He is the same yesterday, today and forever.

## Imitation of the presence

Moses is gone a long time up the mountain. In fact he is gone 40 days and 40 nights – another biblically significant number! This is an intense time. God prescribes the exact details for the tabernacle that He wants Moses to build. The tabernacle is the moveable tent which will house the moving presence of God. The plans include a golden ark, tables, lampstands and more. This is going to take a lot of work. But God is meticulous in what He wants and what will be sufficient as a place for His presence to rest. 40 days, however, was too long for the people of God to wait down at the bottom of the mountain, it seems. If they had not been so fearful to enter in, perhaps things would have been a little different.

This particular mob have very short memories it appears. They are now just three months out of slavery. They moaned about not having any water in the desert, so God found them an oasis called Marah (it had disgusting water, but Moses prayed and miraculously the water was cleansed). Then they find Elim, another oasis with a series of wells. Next they moan about not having enough food and God supernaturally provides them with daily bread and meat. Then they moan once more about the water and Moses causes water to spring from a rock. But now that the pyrotechnics of Mount Sinai are over and Moses has disappeared for a while, the people quickly descend back in boredom and complaining. Frankly, if I was Moses, I would be sick to the back teeth of all their moaning already. Will someone not act with any degree of faith? This is so like the Church. Frankly, we are just moaners much of the time. If we can't experience the presence of God on our terms we become irritable, tired and frustrated. We moan at all the things we don't have, we moan about all the things we do have. Material gain does nothing to satisfy our appetites. Why is it that my kids permanently want to go shopping, but the more they buy the more they whine and moan that they have nothing! It's all part of the wretched human condition. We are made for the presence of God and when we don't get it, we seek to fill the gap in our lives with something, anything that will satisfy that thirst, that hunger, that void. We are beings made for eternity, made for the reality of Heaven, made for the things of His presence. The absence of the tangible presence of God creates a problem. In fact, when there is no presence, we will invariably manufacture something that is an imitation of the presence.

The absence of the presence of God is a dangerous thing for the people of God. We become disillusioned very quickly and seek to "make" something that looks and feels like the presence. The people waiting for Moses got so frustrated that they decided to "make" another god. They reasoned that Moses had disappeared and they need a god to lead them. Even Aaron, the mouthpiece, the priest, buys into this rubbish. So they make a golden calf, a fairly traditional symbol of deity at that time, and start to worship it! They sacrifice to their new deity, they worship it, and in no time at all begin to indulge in "pagan revelry". Astonishing isn't it? Yet even the apostle Peter wanted to create a memorial on the mount of transfiguration to try and "capture the presence" (thankfully Jesus stopped him). We do that. We try to capture the essence of God's presence in some way, try to contain it, and if we can't do that then we create something else to take its place.

This has to be a stark prophetic warning to the Church. Whatever stream, whatever denomination we belong to, we need to ask ourselves, what have we erected that is just a memorial to the past presence of God? Have we begun to worship the memory of past glory rather than experiencing the present glory of His presence? It could be a founding father of our denomination, a past miracle, a past doctrinal revelation, a place where God moved powerfully in the past. It's good to rehearse God's goodness for what He has done, but not at the expense of flowing with the present movement of the Holy Spirit. God has fresh bread for us today. We don't need to cling on to some historic manna which has gone mouldy without us realising it. Can you imagine if the Church of Jesus Christ around the world experienced a fresh outpouring of the presence of God – a fresh living, *current* experience of God? We would find fresh perspectives on the hearts of the founding fathers, we would get repeat miracles, doctrinal treasures would become new in revelation, and places that once experienced the power of God would become centres of outpouring again. Looking to the past has huge benefits only when pursued through the lens of current experiences of God.

The absence of the presence will cause us to worship something else, take away the living experience of God and the result is fatigue, frustration and fear. We will replace God with something else, that you can be certain of. We replace Him with our logic and intellect, with our science and artistic expression, with material things, with the pursuit of experience in all its colour. Without the presence our lives will become a catalogue of chasing one experience after another. If God is not real in our experience then we will pursue what we think is reality, for we must have something to satisfy our quest for the divine.

The absence of the presence leaves our experience cold and meaningless. Our worship becomes routine and dull. The preaching becomes boring. We can live a Christian life outwardly, going through the forms of spirituality, but secretly live another life to satisfy the aching lack of presence. Leaders, do not be fooled. There is no greater priority than to pursue the presence of God. You may have an international ministry, but if you are at the foot of the mountain while the presence seems absent, it won't be long before your ministry becomes your golden calf and you will be worshipping the form and not the Creator.

Fear drives out the presence, but also our frustration and fatigue of waiting for the presence. Turn your waiting into hunger. Turn your fear into godly fear that will keep you from sinning. There is a deception among the people of God, amongst churches that have all the external signs of God's favour, who look like they are presence dwellers, but in fact are building golden calves. The answer is repentance. God's response to Moses was to be done with the people, but Moses turned the heart of God and swept through the camp cleansing it. Similarly, we need to repent and direct our hunger and thirst towards the mighty presence of God once again.

## Endnotes

67. Colossians 3:2
68. Ephesians 2:8; Romans 1:17; Hebrews 11:6
69. 1 John 4:18
70. Exodus 19
71. Exodus 20:20

# Glory

CHAPTER

7

"Glory is the sum total of God's attributes …
it is the nearest we come to describing God in one word."
—*RT Kendall* [72]

In the UK we have a day when we remember those who have died in past and present wars. It is a day of solemnity, memorial and glory. We glory in the achievements and sacrifice of our brave armed forces who fought to win freedom for the rest of the population. Similarly, we glory in the sporting achievements of our Olympic athletes or favoured sporting teams. We refer to restoring buildings to their "former glory". As Christians we sing to bring glory to God and we ask Him to display His glory. But what exactly is "glory"?

Scripture reveals a seriousness and weightiness to the concept of glory that makes it clear it is not something to be trifled with. The Hebrew word for it – *kabod* – is infused with meaning: quantity, weightiness, significance, abundance. Glory is something that is heavy and awesome. It is not to be messed with; it is not a trivial phrase that should just fall off our tongues.

Glory is the ultimate revelation of the fullness of God. It is His essence. It is the single word that most sums up God's awesome character – if it were possible to use just one word as RT

Kendall rightly points out. We say "glory" because within the limits of our human expression we are fumbling to quantify the essential spiritual nature of God. Glory is also literally the honour due to God, as well as Who He is – the "visible manifestation of the excellence of God's character" [73].

God reveals His nature by His actions, just as we all do. Whenever we do something, we naturally disclose certain aspects our nature. A generous person will be liberal with positive comments and give materially to others. A selfish person will be stingy both in word and action. A happy person will exude joy and a miserable person will create a negative atmosphere. I recently read a report from some friends who have left the UK to work with children in Africa and their words reveal the heart they have for the orphaned. What they are doing reflects who they are. We cannot help but display who we are. So it is with God. He constantly displays who He is. He manifests Himself in all He does and we call this expression His *glory*.

John used the Greek word for glory, *doxa*, when referring to Jesus. *Doxa* means "praise, honour, worship, dignity, a good opinion". So we get this phrase,

*"So the Word became human and made his home among us. He was full of unfailing love and faithfulness. And we have seen his glory, the glory of the Father's one and only Son."* (John 1:14)

John is saying that such is Christ's authority as an ambassador of the Father, that if we have seen His glory, we have as good as seen the Father's glory.

Britain has embassies all around the world, like any sovereign country. Each embassy has an ambassador who is the representative of Great Britain wherever they are. In fact, each embassy is considered a literal "piece" of Great Britain. Our ambassadors are backed with the full force of the British Government, so that when you meet with one, it is as good as meeting with the Government in Westminster. The authority of the Government is invested in these people and we would probably go to war for the sake of one of them. In one person the "glory" of the British Government (you may laugh at the idea of Britain having glory, but surely it can be a Great nation once again) is invested. In the same way, all the glory of the Father was invested in Jesus Christ. In Jesus we *see* the glory of God manifest. Jesus the *logos* word of God has made visible the *doxa* glory of God. Jesus revealed to us the nature of the Father. It is difficult to get our heads around the concept, because it is ultimately a spiritual phenomenon and any attempt to fathom the divine nature will only ever limit the depth of the character of God as we approach it with our flawed words.

## Glory breaks out

Before Jesus did any miracle, before He healed anyone, before He was a somebody, the glory of God broke out. Remember that Christmassy night when the farmers were out doing their job, looking after the livestock, enjoying a cup of tea (if they were English!) and the Chief angel lit up the night sky with the glory of the Lord and frightened them to death? The radiance of the divine nature literally spilled out in physical light to herald the impending arrival of the Messiah. Glory was expressed in incredible, piercing light.

Hebrews describes Jesus as *radiating* this glory[74], like a radiator in your house which pours out a heat that fills the entire space. Jesus constantly poured out the very essence and nature of God. It was invisible to the eye, yet people felt the effects of the glory! Jesus grew up and went about doing stuff and in time was prepared by God for His ministry. His first miracle, turning water into wine, is described as a demonstration of the glory of God.[75] The fact is, when God is about, He cannot help but make impossibilities possible. Wherever there is lack, the glory of God brings abundance. Later when Jesus raised Lazarus from the dead, it was another display of God's glorious nature – a God who can bring life from death, a God who cannot abide death so resurrection is part of His essence. Indeed, it was the glory of God that brought Jesus back to life.[76] When the glory is present, life happens, creativity happens, inspiration happens. It's not surprising then that we read accounts in the Bible of people pursuing the glory of God. If we can stand it, the glory is fantastic, something that, experienced with our spiritual and natural senses, makes us exclaim, "Wow!"

## Pursuing glory

Let's return to following Moses' story. He had his God encounter with a shrub that was on fire. Could it have been the visible brightness of God's glory – a searing, burning light that engulfed but did not consume?

God promised that when His people were free from their captivity in Egypt, He would bring them to the mountain so that they could make sacrifice and worship Him. This is exactly what He did. Then Moses, under very specific instructions from God, spent some time going up and down the mountain communicating with the people of His behalf. The climax of this event was that God decided to present Moses with the Law – the set of principles which reflected the glory of God. These were rules to lay boundary lines which helped us live closer to that which was intended for us. The Law was very much second best to the indwelling power of the Spirit which was to come.

Moses, brimming with these words from Heaven, is greeted by a lot of enthusiasm from the people – after all, after many years in captivity God is doing amazing things and finally speaking to *His people*. Moses effectively got out his laptop (Keiller translation) and wrote down the exact words down God spoke. After making a sacrifice, his key leadership team and seventy elders of the tribes of Israel went up the mountain.

This was an incredible time. They saw God standing on what appeared to be a sheet of blue glass – feeble words to describe a heavenly sight. They didn't get zapped as some feared, but rather God prepared an amazing banquet. While they were tucking into this incredible feast God spoke: "I've written out my instructions for you Moses, come up here and get them."

Moses with his intern, Joshua, didn't waste any time in going higher up the mountain. As they went up, a cloud appeared and covered the mountain; they were walking into a dense fog. As this cloud hovered over the rocks, the *"glory of the Lord settled down"*[77] Wow! The very essence of God descended on this wilderness mountain. What was Moses to do? Nothing, he just waited by the cloud for six days. Can you imagine, he just hung around the glory for six days? There is no mention of eating or going to the loo! The very presence of God was literally on that rock, so Moses was going nowhere until he was released to do so. Then, on the day of rest, the Sabbath, Moses hears God calling him. We don't know exactly what was said, but there was an invitation to come into the very nature and presence of God. "Hey Moses, do you want to experience my nature? Do you want to feel my essence? Do you want to understand me with your spirit? Then come into the cloud. Don't worry, you wont be burnt to a crisp, you have sat there for six days, you are soaked in the presence now." The Israelites, back at the boundary line, could only see a raging fire. "Nothing can survive that," they thought. "Moses is toast." The appearance of the glory from a distance was as fire, but up close it was like a cloud.

### Tabernacle

Moses stayed immersed in the presence of the Living God for forty days – the number of days it rained on Noah's ark; the number of days that Jesus was tempted in the wilderness; the number of days Jesus appeared alive after He was resurrected. We read of Moses' encounter with God. He was taught and instructed on what was next for the people of God: the creation of the tabernacle.

Over the course of the next five weeks, God gave Moses a blueprint for a tabernacle. Its purpose was so that God could live among them.[78] This was God making His plans to be ever present with His beloved people. As had just been demonstrated, the people would not survive if God in all His holiness just appeared, so God puts forth a way in which it can be possible to dwell amongst them.

There was a trinity of parts to the temple. The outer court-yard contained the Altar, the place of sacrifice, where people were confronted by their need for repentance and for a substitute to bear the price of their sin, made on their behalf by a gate-keeper to God. Next the Holy place, nearer to God, a place separated by priests who were only able to enter once a day to offer a sacrifice. It was a place of reverence, a place which needed to be kept pure. Finally came the Most Holy Place or Holy of Holies. This was the actual place where God touched earth, the very dwelling place of God, where God lived, His house! This was the place of *glory*. Entrance to this place was permitted to the very senior priest only, and then only once a year.

*"You shall put the mercy seat on the top of the ark, and in the ark you shall put the Testimony* [the Ten Commandments] *that I will give you. There I will meet with you and, from above the mercy seat, from between the two cherubim that are upon the ark of the Testimony, I will speak intimately with you of all which I will give you in commandment to the Israelites."* (Exodus 25:21-22 Amplified Bible)

## God meets man

Right there in the most precious place of all we find the place of mercy. If you haven't got the picture yet, dealing with God's presence is no light matter, this is life and death stuff. Entering the tabernacle to engage with God is like handling radioactive material – you need to be incredibly careful and treat it with extreme caution. Here, in the Most Holy Place, is where the ultimate act of divine reconciliation and grace takes place, where God draws lost people to Himself; where He makes "at one" by an offering of blood those who were once alienated.[79] The theme of blood makes its finale with the blood of Jesus.[80] The Mercy Seat is the place of intimacy with the Father. It is in this place, once a year, that God gets the sort of relationship He really wants with His people: an intimate union, where man is not saddled with the blockages of sin, but rather he can be himself, just like the days when Adam walked with God in the garden.

The Ark of Testimony or witness (eventually to become known as the Ark of the Covenant or Promise), had in it the tablets of stone (the Ten Commandments), the gold jar of Manna and Aaron's staff that budded.[81] These elements represented the stories that shaped this unique people. Rightly they were called "testimony" because they recalled the supernatural dealings of God with His people: the word of God divinely revealed on the mountain in front of the people; God instructing His people; the incredible food provision in the desert and God caring for His people; the rod that saw the miraculous flight from tyranny as God gave His people an escape route. We would do well to reflect on how lightly we sometimes treat our own stories of God's faithfulness; our story of His salvation; the times when He healed us or provided for us or gave us a second chance. In our desire for immediacy we can consume the wonders of God like we consume everything else around us – the problem we face living in a consumer society! We need to rethink the way we reflect on the story of the Church, of God's dealings with us, of His wonders. We need to record and share the stories of God moving amongst us, for in them the presence of God chooses to dwell.

The Tabernacle was no palace. Rather it was a tent. The people of God were not a settled people, they were a people on the move, roaming the desert at the leading of God. It took a long time to get the Tabernacle constructed, so in the meantime they made a temporary structure. When they stopped they would erect a Tent of Meeting, where God could meet with man. Moses would enter the tent[82] and the whole nation would stand and watch him from the entrances of their own tents. This was a spectacle every time. When Moses entered a column of cloud came down and all the time that God was talking that glory cloud hovered over the tent. In this place, there was intimate conversation. This was not the booming judgement of God; God would speak to Moses *"as a man speaks with his friend."*[83] "Hi Moses. How's it going? How are the people doing? … I know … it's hard, isn't it? … Don't let them get you down … You know I'm with you … I love you …." The story of Moses is steeped in pyrotechnics, fire and smoke, loud voices, booming commands. But when all the right elements are in place, all the boundaries set up, the Tabernacle erected exactly as it should be, then God is finally able to relate with Moses as He did with Adam. Formality taken care of, God can show His true nature, His essence. There, between the angelic guard either side of the Mercy Seat, above the symbols telling the story of God's dealings with man, the place where the blood was spilled, God presenced Himself. Angels … story … blood … the meeting place of God and man.

## Show us your glory!

Then we get the cry of Moses to God: "Never leave us God! In fact, if you don't go with us where ever we go, then we are staying still." [84] People of God today, this must be our cry: "God, don't leave us! We need You! We can't do this without You!" Have we become so professional, so slick at what we do, so clever in our running of church that we don't need God? Moses had learned that no matter how great a leader he was, there was no point unless God was with them. Thankfully, God responded to Moses' petition and agreed to go, not just with Moses but also the people of God. Audacious Moses, giving the Almighty an ultimatum! But then directness, boldness and honesty are qualities of the best friendships. Then Moses makes a further audacious request. He asks God to show him His glory. Have we lost the cry of Moses, "Show me your glory"? Moses had a desperation for more of the presence of God. He wanted more of God's nature to be revealed, to understand more of His essence. Our cry should similarly be, "Show us Your glory!" We need to be hungry, desperate for the presence of God to light up our lives, to shine into the darkness of our troubled world. We need to unleash a glory cloud of fire on our nation once again. Our pearl hunt seeks out glory!

Moses finished the Tabernacle according to the pattern God had given him and this replaced the Tent of Meeting. When it was finished, the glory of God filled the newly completed structure. God had come to stay. [85] Rather than making an occasional visit, God had begun something new: permanent residence with His people. God had moved into the neighbourhood and a permanent presence was established.

## Temple

Of course, the tabernacle was merely a shadow of something that was to come. God's real intention was never to create a temporary or a fixed structure to house His presence. His true desire was to relate with man directly. Relationships are not about buildings, they are about an intimate and emotional connection. Moses was a friend of God, so it is not surprising that another man called "friend of God" wanted to build a permanent residence for God – David.

We fast-forward in time. David has taken the throne and is the undisputed king over all Israel. He brings the Ark of the Covenant, that symbol of the presence of God, to Jerusalem.[86] David is getting used to the pleasures and privileges of kingship and he enjoys the palace and all the luxuries it offers. No one is fighting Israel, there is peace in the nation. Here is a man who has lived from cave to cave and on horseback for years, now relaxing with all that the world has to offer. But what about the presence of God? What about the Ark? How can David enjoy these pleasures when the very presence of God is stuck in a tent outside the palace? David is not happy with this. He wants to build a palace for God – a temple.

God speaks to David[87] and gives him the vision of a permanent dwelling place for God on a grander scale than the Tabernacle. In the same way that the people of God have found their home, it is fitting that God has His permanent home among them. There is both a fixed and moveable nature to the presence of God: fixed in the sense that He will never leave us, and yet moveable in that the presence of God moves like the wind. Unfortunately, through personal sin David forfeits the right to build God's temple himself and the responsibility falls to his son, Solomon.

Renowned for his wisdom, Solomon was a great choice for building the temple. David's vision for a permanent house for God would be fulfilled. It was constructed according to the same pattern as the Tabernacle – more lavish, more splendid, but essentially the same idea. When the building is finally completed they bring in the Ark, God falls in glory on that place and spiritual carnage ensues. The priests stagger all over the place, some falling over, some completely zonked – all due to the dense glory cloud again. The presence of God was thick in the temple.[88] During the dedication ceremony Solomon reaches the end of his prayers and the fire of God comes roaring down from Heaven and gobbles up the sacrificial offering. The glory of God was so overwhelming in that place that the priests couldn't get through the door! The glory was so weighty that they would just keep falling over. With all this fire and visible glory it is not surprising that the assembled crowd hit the deck and started worshiping, declaring their love for God. That is what happens when the glory presence of God is around: there is worship and the nature of God is declared – the words *"goodness and love lasts forever"* was sung and sung.

The glory breaking out in visible form is what we want to see today. Bring it on! God has not finished with such events. I have been in enough gatherings of the people of God to know that He still deals with us in this way. We no longer need the priesthood to intervene on our behalf, because we are all priests. We don't need to erect any special places because *we are* walking tabernacles of God. David's vision of a temple has been recast with new language, perhaps in a way which David, the man of relationship, would have preferred.

*"Together, we are his house, built on the foundation of the apostles and the prophets. And the cornerstone is Christ Jesus himself. We are carefully joined together in him, becoming a holy temple for the Lord. Through him you Gentiles are also being made part of this dwelling where God lives by his Spirit."* (Ephesians 2:20-22 NLT)

We are a brick by brick temple for the Lord. The apostolic and prophetic gift provides a foundation to this new, exciting temple (it is interesting that the presence of God comes not with the "roof" of the apostolic, but with it as a "foundation".) Apostles and Prophets provide the floor for the bricks to be laid on, they are not supposed to lead by command and control, but lead by humbly serving. The Apostles and Prophets must be the guardians of the collective stories, the protectors of the tablets of truth, the providers of fresh manna, the people whose rod releases the people from captivity. Jesus is the cornerstone of this new temple. He is the cement that joins us together. It will all fall over without Him. This assembly of the glorious temple is going to take time, but God can wait, He is in no hurry. He wants an awesome temple that far outstrips any earthly copy. The spiritual, authentic article will take time to complete – every brick from every denomination carefully honed and stuck together.

## We are given glory

God didn't need to create man because He was lonely, rather man was created for the glory of God.[89] We are part of the display of the very nature and essence of God.

The twenty four elders in the book of Revelation declare the glory belonging to God.[90]

Jesus prayed to His Father in Heaven, *"I brought glory to you here on earth by completing the work you gave me to do. Now, Father, bring me into the glory we shared before the world began."* [91]

Jesus had a wonderful existence with the Father before man was ever created, and clearly He gave this up to come to earth as a man. But look: Jesus in his human clothing brings glory back to God. He fulfilled the purpose for which He was sent and demonstrated to all mankind that we too can bring glory to God. Look how Jesus prays for us, His Church to come:

*"I have given them the glory you gave me, so they may be one as we are one. I am in them and you are in me. May they experience such perfect unity that the world will know that you sent me and that you love them as much as you love me. Father, I want these whom you have given me to be with me where I am. Then they*

*can see all the glory you gave me because you loved me even before*
*the world began!"* (John 17: 22-24)

Mankind is given God's glory like an inheritance. We are
passed the baton by Christ. He modelled something for us to
follow. He lived His life to fulfil His purpose – glorifying God.
Now it's our turn. Now we have the opportunity to glorify
God and experience true unity. The same unity that the Trinity
enjoy is open to us. The wonderful expectation for the Church
is that it will be able to experience a unique oneness. Can you
imagine a Church that is truly one? That is the prayer of the
Saviour of mankind. But He doesn't stop at that thought, Jesus
wants the Church to be brought into complete unity with God
in the Heavenly realms – wow! Get your head around that. Or
rather, get your spirit around that!

Our purpose on Earth is literally to be the glory of God.
That is why we are slowly but surely being transformed *"from*
*one degree of glory to another"*.[92] God is shaping us, crafting us,
giving us glimpses of His glory and leading us to a deeper
revelation of glory. I don't know whether you have grasped this
or not … but it means *you!* You have the glory inside of you. If
you are baptised in the Holy Spirit you are stuffed full of glory.
All those pictures of tents and temples are just a shadow of the
spiritual reality of what God has done and is doing in you.
Jesus has transferred all the divine essence into us – the power
now emanating from the residing Holy Spirit in us.

This is a truly awesome revelation. We get to work out this
glory day by day. We get to revel in the presence. We get to
experience what Moses experienced. Inside you right now is
the nature of God, the complete character of God. You get the
fun of going from one level of glory to another level of glory.
Don't kid yourself, however. If you mess around with sin then
the glory is going to leak out.[93] Don't be under any illusion that
dark and light can occupy the same space. However, you can

meet God again at the mercy seat, the place where the blood is sprinkled. You can come to get mercy from God, not once a year, but whenever you need it. Relationship is restored, heavenly unity is the theme, the unity of the Trinity united with the unity of the Church.

## The Church is the glory of God on earth

And so the story of the temple continues, God now dwelling in His people. We have sought to internalise much of the presence of God and make it a personal experience. It is, of course, a personal experience, but it is so much more. We are temples, but also bricks of this glorious house. Glory to glory. The revelation of our personal salvation is glory, the idea of the Church of Jesus being the temple is glory to an even greater glory. We will often confine our experience of God to a personal time with Him or a meeting of the church, but God is interested in depositing so much more of His glory in His Church.

What about times of corporate praise and worship which are so intense you feel as if fire could fall or a thick cloud appear?

What about taking the glory that is in you into your homes, sharing it with your neighbours in crisis, the lonely in your street who find they are attracted to you and the band of believers that meet with you?

What about the glory that will go with you to work, the glory that dwells in you on the train?

We have an incredible capacity to hold the glory of God and give it away. Why do we get consumed with what we can get out of it, rather than be filled with the feeling that this is a glory that will attract, a glory that will change people, a glory that is God's very essence on earth?

When we begin to compare the old ways of glory, the Moses glory, the stuff of the past, it is really nothing in comparison to the wonderful presence of God now. We have got a glory that starts now and continues forever.[94] When we start to live in the reality of this power, this divine nature, then we become emboldened; we have an incredible everlasting hope. There is literally a transformation taking place in us. The presence of God changes us, it takes away the barrier, the veil, and releases us into a freedom.[95] We are to reflect the nature of God to all around.

Let's raise our expectation, let's cry, "Come, Lord Jesus!" Let the reality of Heaven impact us because God has made His dwelling place with us. God has moved in and brought with Him all the privileges and blessings of Heaven.

## Endnotes

72. Understanding Theology Vol 1, RT Kendall, Christian Focus Publications p64.
73. Wayne Grudem, Systematic Theology, IVP.
74. Hebrews 1:3
75. John 22:11
76. Romans 6:4
77. Exodus 24:16
78. Exodus 25:8
79. Leviticus 17:11
80. Romans 3:25, 1 John 2:2
81. Hebrews 9:4
82. Exodus 33:7-8
83. Exodus 33:11
84. Exodus 33:12-23
85. Exodus 40:34-38
86. 2 Samuel 6
87. 2 Samuel 7
88. 1 Kings 8:10-11
89. Isaiah 43:7
90. Revelation 4:11
91. John 17:4-5
92. 2 Corinthians 3:18, Amplified Bible
93. Proverbs 26:1, Kabod "glory" translated "Honour".
94. 2 Corinthians 3:10-11
95. 2 Corinthians 3:16-18

# Holy, Holy, Holy

For a moment, let's peer into Heaven and see one man's encounter with holiness – the young Isaiah.[96]

*Words of prophetic declaration, "Holy, holy, holy" shook the sanctuary of the heavenly palace like an earthquake, yet the throne room didn't fall down. Smoke filled the room like it was on fire. It was overwhelming; it was beyond understanding. The prophet could not stand the awesome scene any more. He screamed as if it was his last breath, "It's over!" The prophet had glimpsed his sinfulness at that moment; the holiness of the scene crashed into the dirt of his mortality. The wreckage of his emotions was confusion, devastation, a deep knowing of his sinful state next to white majesty of God. Why wasn't he brushed aside with a fiery breath? Why was he still alive? Surely the stain of his life could not remain in the presence of God?*

*One of the mighty attendants came towards the young prophet with a burning coal from the altar. It was bright and hot, burning with the glory of God. A black coal from the mines of earth had been so infused with glory that it shone brightly – something dark and hard had been trans-formed into a container of the glory. So it was possible, darkness*

*could be changed into a light carrier. The hot coal flew at the*
*prophet and hit his mouth. The prophet now became the very*
*carrier of light and glory, just as the coal had been, in an*
*instantaneous transferral of power. The King's servant*
*decreed, "You are no longer guilty, you are forgiven."*
*Redemption and acceptance now flowed into the prophet,*
*prostrate on the floor. The darkness and heaviness that had*
*confronted him only a moment ago had vanished. This was a*
*new start, a wiping of the slate!*

Holy encounters are the stuff of changed lives. When we con-
front true holiness we find we have to face our sinful state and
the result is a moment of wretchedness as we realise how black
and messed up we are!

I don't mind letting you into a secret. I struggle with the
concept of the holiness of God. I think that my emphasis has
been on God's grace, His love, His Father's heart, His kindness.
In a way, I have cherry picked the qualities of God that I have
needed to hear and feel. All of them have been true, but I commit
a form of heresy if I cannot hold in tension the holiness of God
with the love of God. It is precisely because of His holiness that
I can be wholly loved! But just to excuse my heresy for a
minute, there are mitigating circumstances. I have found over
my thirty years of Christian experience that those believers
who emphasise the holiness of God over everything else tend
to be dull, boring killjoys who are strict, legalistic and severe.
Holiness freaks tend to see sin in everything, a devil in every
bush, and think that any contact with anything remotely
worldly is evil! Is it any surprise that I run a mile from them,
that they make me feel unworthy, sinful and judged? Believers
can do that fairly easily: make others feel like rubbish. As
Christians we have an uncanny knack of coming across as
superior and enlightened, like spiritual school teachers looking
down our noses at the dreadful state of others. I am exaggerating

(slightly) for effect, but that is the sense I have. My equally wrong reaction is to run a mile and fall into the error of cheap grace – that all is forgiven, all done on the cross, the Father loves me anyway, whatever I do!

As I start to explore the presence of God, I find myself in an inescapable vortex. I am sucked into the inevitable end that when I am dealing with God I am dealing with a *Holy God.* I can't escape the truth that God has an "otherness" quality – He is not like me. I agree with the Old Testament character Hannah when she says, "No one is holy like the Lord." [97] No one indeed. I don't want God to be holy, in the fearful wrathful sense of the word. I want Him to be a benign Granddad who plays with me, smiles at me, has the faint smell of pipe tobacco masked by the smell of mints, and looks like a permanently happy Santa Clause. That is what I *think* I want, at least, someone accessible, friendly and stable. But the God of the Bible doesn't conform to that rather narrow interpretation. He has some frightening personality features which we can try to edit out of our Bibles, or theologically explain away, yet they are still there.

I think that we really don't get the idea of holiness – at least, I don't think I have. But to experience the enduring presence of God is to come face to face with His holiness. Holiness strips away all the pretence, all the masks we wear. It is the undiluted force of the nature of God – God full on and in your face!

## God is holy

So lets grapple with it. Holiness is moral uprightness, divine transcendence, God's uniqueness. It means, in the Hebrew, "to set apart, make distinct, put at a distance from". The word seems to be interchangeably used with sanctification and saint. It is about the sacred, the things that belong to God. Holy is a word used to show that something belongs to Him.

One of the rituals involved in being a parent is sewing name tags in the backs of jumpers and PE kits for your kids. I still remember the proud moment of seeing my name sewn into my school shirt. It spoke of something that belonged only to me. "Holy" is like that for God. What God calls holy is holy![98] The list in the Bible makes interesting reading: Holy Spirit, holy place, holy people, holy city, holy man, holy angels, holy prophets, holy covenant, holy one of God, holy Father, holy servant Jesus, holy ground, holy Scriptures, holy kiss, holy nation, holy women. Anything to do with God is holy! Holiness is the very state of God, part of His nature, part of His essential being. In the same way that glory is the external expression of God, holiness can be viewed as the depth of His character. My public face, my preaching, my dealings with others, my perceived character is my "glory" – the outward manifestation of who I am. By contrast, my secret inner life, my private journey, my thoughts are "holy" (well, not that holy I must confess!) Do you get the point?

In our pursuit of the presence of God we not only want to experience the external radiance of His glory, but also become intimate with the essential nature of His Holiness. Purity and cleanliness is not holiness. "Cleanness is a condition of holiness, not holiness itself."[99] Wayne Grudem puts it this way: "God's holiness means that He is separated from sin and devoted to seeking His own honour." At first it sounds selfish for God to seek His own honour, but it can't be, as that would be sin and therefore unholy.

"God is holy"[100], the Seraphim angels declare it[101], the psalmist sings it.[102] His holiness is displayed by His righteousness[103]. R. T. Kendall says, "There is no earthly frame of reference by which we can fully understand God ... God is wholly other as some theologians have put it. This means that God is utterly different from what man is and does." Stanley Grenz ranks holiness as, "among the fundamental moral attributes of God." Much like the word glory, it seems as though "holy" is a word used to sum up something that cannot be readily expressed or explained – a word so full of meaning yet whose meaning is still veiled; a word that is at the same time unattainable and yet the end goal of our pursuit. Holiness is the part of the character of God that is the destiny for mankind. He is holy and that is what we are supposed to be.

We cannot get far in our hunger for God, in our search for understanding, in our pursuit of His presence unless we are arrested by the fact that we are talking about a holy God. It is not really surprising that in the throne room the best the angels can think of to sing is, "Holy, holy, holy ..." It seems to be the only word that can capture the uniqueness, the loftiness, the awesome terror of God!

## Getting to grips with holiness

Holiness has connotations of majesty. When we speak of God being holy, we are also describing the royalty and pomp of a King dressed in incredible beauty. The movie *The Young Victoria* came out recently, documenting the early life of Queen Victoria. There were some breathtaking scenes of her coronation in that film, with the trumpets blasting, the ermine fringed red robe, the golden sceptre, the jewel-studded orb and finally the magnificent crown of state. It was a truly "holy" event! We get an idea of what holiness looks like in such a moment – the sense of significance, the importance of the event. If some normal person, dressed in normal clothes had entered Westminster Abbey, it would have looked so incongruous, so bizarre, just plain wrong!

Holiness is the perfection of the sovereignty of God, His rule, His authority. Holiness is special, set apart, distinct. God tells us Himself in the Ten Commandments that He is a "jealous

God" [104] – at first, a strange character trait to ascribe to Himself. If I was to declare that I am a jealous man, most would understand this as a character flaw, rather than a godly trait, but when used of God it takes on a holiness. In this context it refers to an incredible zeal for His people. God simply cannot stand for His people, His creation, to set their affection on anything other than Himself. God is as jealous as a lover, after all He is the Groom and we are the Bride. What groom is not jealous for the affections of his bride? If a bride flirts with another man, don't you think that the groom will get more than a bit jealous? Jealousy for our affection is part of the holy nature of God. He cannot abide His creation expressing affection for any other god.

Righteousness is the expression of holiness. Holiness is more than just "right living". Right living is the *consequence* of holiness, though to put holiness in the same category as human goodness is to devalue it. God is right all the time, He is never wrong, never lies, never tells a half truth; He is always in the right and acts out of righteousness. So if there is something that seems odd in the way God behaves, it must be our understanding that is wrong because He is the plumb line of righteousness. In a world where righteousness is seen as subjective, where everyone has the opportunity to create their own truth, where it is wrong to tell someone they are wrong and where absolute truth is diluted to personal opinion, we can still declare that God is true and righteous in all He does. The angels and believers in Heaven sing about God: *"For you alone are holy ... for your righteous acts have been revealed."* [105] God displays His holiness in his actions.

Because God's holiness is righteous He is concerned about justice. God is always fair and equitable with His creation. He is not biased or vindictive, but just. He will one day judge every creature against His righteous standard. He is the rule maker and will measure us against these rules. We cannot dismiss the judgement of God just because it makes us feel uncomfortable. Judgement is an essential part of the golden thread of grace that weaves it way through Scripture. We miss the truly amazing nature of the grace of God if we do not embrace the justice of God. When we talk about justice we need to talk about wrath, the anger of God visited on those who break His commands, who transgress His holiness. We cannot see anger and wrath as an uncontrolled emotional outburst which lashes out against us. Rather, the wrath of God is the full force of the Law being exercised when we are found guilty. It is the fire wall of God that burns against anything that seeks to compromise the purity of His holiness.

I hate writing this, because I am a grace man; I have found favour in God's eyes which is totally undeserving; yet the wrath of God is real. As a father of children whom I adore, I would do anything for them, go anywhere for them, would give my life for them. But there have been times when I have burned with anger because they have offended or stepped over the line. Do I love them still? Always. But please don't wrap the holiness of God up in cotton wool. God will defy our attempts to tame Him. He is ultimately the wild Lion of Judah who will never be caged despite our feeble attempts to understand Him. Our world needs to see the true force of a roaring lion, not just the purr of a pussy cat! Isaiah found out that God was holy when he declared that he was "undone" because he had seen the ferocious holiness of the King. Uzzah met with his death as a result of lending a hand to stop the Ark of the Covenant falling into the mud – was this fair or holy? What is our feeble definition of fairness compared to the awesome power of God's holiness? Mankind needs to get over itself. We arrogantly try to define God and apply our own debased, compromised standard to the powerful might of the Living God.

Tozer describes the moment of confronting God's holiness as "emotionally violent" for the suppliant. He goes on to remark, "We know nothing like the divine holiness. It stands apart, unique, unapproachable, incomprehensible and unattainable. The natural man is blind to it. He may fear God's power and admire His wisdom, but His holiness he cannot even imagine." Society is blinded to the nature of holiness. We have recalibrated the "right" and "wrong" of our laws to suit the democratic standards of society. We are not interested in the divine standard. That which provided the foundations of our society hundreds of years ago – an attempt to live out the standards of heavenly righteousness – has slowly been eroded and undermined by secular atheism until it is a shadow of its former glory. Who we have sex with is no longer the prerogative of the law – we have the right to choose. Women can exercise the choice to determine whether their unborn children live or not. Increasingly, individual adults are deciding to die at the moment of their choosing. It's all about "personal choice". Personal choice is the new age warped definition of holiness. We have become gods in our own eyes and the only "sin" we know of is that of transgressing our free will. This is why any religious or moral code is repugnant to the secular social justice movement. Any attempt to curtail our "right" is an abuse. The divine has been reduced to the confines of the temple of our souls. No longer are we subject to an external deity, we are simply the god's of our own destiny.

For me, Tozer grasps the importance of the divine holy:

"In the study of the holy it can never be intellectually conceived, only sensed and felt in the depths of the human spirit. It remains as a permanent religious instinct, a feeling for that unnamed, undiscoverable presence that runs quicksilver-like through creation's veins and sometimes stuns the mind by confronting it with a supernatural, supra-rational manifestation of itself. The man thus confronted is brought down and over-whelmed and can only tremble and be silent."

In other words, a dose of the gob smacking confrontation of holiness is what our western world needs to jolt it out of either passivity or arrogance. When the holiness of God confronts the western mind we will fall to our feet, stunned by the majestic righteousness of God. Revival should be ushered in with a message of holy love, extravagant love and majestic holiness. It needs to start by reviving those passive, defeated believers who have lost the wonder of the holiness of God and struggle to make sense of faith. Wake up and seek the holy justice of God! Bow your knee to the might of God! The very answer to the sickness of our society is a return to the health of holiness. In fact, the Anglo-Saxon word for "holy" derives from *halig* or *hal* meaning "well" or "whole". If we want a whole society then we must be pursuers of holiness. The hatred of God for sin is not a hatred of people, but rather a hatred of the causes of sickness and sinfulness. God is extreme as a jealous lover for His people; extreme enough to judge the world. More Tozer: "Holy is the way God is. To be holy He does not conform to a standard. He is that standard. He is absolutely holy with an infinite, incom-prehensible fullness of purity that is incapable of being other than it is."

The holiness of God is incomparable[106] to anything we know, unapproachable[107] without fear of death, is in utter contrast to man[108], and is literally exalted and sublime[109]. To quote God Himself, "I am holy ..."[110] It says it all really!

## The drama of the holy

The story of the people of God in the Old Testament is a drama of man's wrestle with the holiness of the divine. God is clear that He will, after all, abide with mankind, but in order for that to work He must protect his Holiness. He cannot live with man unless He can be true to Himself, so He must protect His nature or else He will kill humanity! The design God gave to Moses then, was a campus that ensured the holiness of God was diffused sufficiently so that, at worst, mankind might get "sunburned" by the presence of God, rather than incinerated by its glory. The temple's design was such that the outer rooms were less intense than the inner rooms in terms of experiencing the presence. Each compartment was like a divine "fire wall" and the closer you got to the inner sanctum, the holier it became. Approaching the Holy of Holies had to be done with extreme caution, otherwise one would not live to tell the tale. Uzzah's demise was a vivid demonstration of the drama of holiness. How many of us have sought to give God a hand, rather than respect His way of doing things?

The drama of the temple meant that you could "not simply barge in upon the holy one"[111]; you had to wait until you were allowed in. Queen Esther demonstrates this idea so brilliantly. Burdened by the plight of her people, the Jews, she is sent on a mission to persuade her husband, King Xerxes. She waits nervously at the outer courtyard until the king offers his sceptre as a sign that he will allow her to approach. The holiness of the scene is conveyed by the fact that she cannot simply walk in and make her request – she has to bide her time and wait. I have a very healthy concept of the King of kings being my "Dad", and generally Dad's just allow their kids access to them whenever. As I write, my little girl has just walked into my study, thrown her arms around my neck and said goodnight. The door was closed because I was writing, but she knows she has an invitation to come in because I'm at home, and that's what we do at home. What if I had been at the office? It's not uncommon for me to go from one confidential meeting to another, so would it have been appropriate for her to rush in? Of course not.

How often do we stop to consider the absolute holiness of God? I do wonder if we Spirit-filled-clapping-cappuccino-drinking-river-types barge into the holy places of God with little awareness of what He is presently engaged with. Yes, there are moments when God is Daddy, but also where God is GOD! He is the same, yet He is different. To stretch this analogy a little further: if my little girl did rush in and kiss me, the person I was talking to may just find this cute. I apologise and then we would carry on. But if she was a fully-grown adult, the person might feel it was an insensitive and inappropriate intrusion and be offended. We need to strike a balance: to be childlike enough to rush without inhibition into the arms of our Heavenly Daddy, but mature enough to sense Him working in His holiness and to approach with caution and an awesome respect. This is how I see things – or perhaps I just don't fully get the lavish nature of the grace of God? Well, I am journeying. I offer these thoughts as feeble attempt to get to grips with mystery.

Eugene Peterson says, "the tabernacle represented God's holy presence in the midst of His people and His rule over them." Presence and rule. It is still true today: God's presence is in us and He expresses His rule through us. These images of the tabernacle, which turned into a temple, which was then referred to as the City of God or Mount Zion, are all images of the dwelling of the presence of God with mankind. We carry the reality of the presence in us every day and are being built together as living blocks of stone to create the new temple – the Church![112]

The drama of holiness is played out in the organisation of our week. The idea of keeping one day free from the ordinary was the idea of the Sabbath.[113] There is still truth in the principle, though perhaps we are not so legalistic about it now and see it as common sense, freeing ourselves from the relentless pressures of work. Yes, though we are supposedly free and have so much free time, we seem more stressed and anxious than ever before. The psalmist has the right idea when he wrote, *"It is useless for you to work so hard from early morning until late at night, anxiously working for food to eat; for God gives rest to his loved ones."*[114] Our rest days are holy, our holi-days are holy! Rest gives place to peace which is a dynamic of Heaven.

## A loving holiness

Bruner talks about the "paradoxical dualism" of holiness and love: the idea that wrathful, holy justice sits side by side with the passionate love of God. "The presence of sin transforms the experience of the divine love from the bliss intended by God into wrath,"[115] writes Grenz. Sin is a wrecker; it erodes the intended life like a vicious cancer eating away at the body. The nature of God is to invite His creation into holy communion with Him, to look at the created order and say "it is good" – a physical creation made holy in the very image of God. But most of the story of God's dealings with man is the quest to restore relationship that ends in an eternal peace. Even when the gap is healed and the holy love of God can flow unrestricted to the hungry hearts of man, the tension still remains between a holy God and a loving God. God cannot break the standard of His nature – He cannot become unholy – yet He relates unconditionally to human sinfulness. Of course, this is the dilemma that Jesus went through, the reconciliation of man to God, the spanning of the divide between holy God and sinful man. You can feel the full force of this painful tension in the pilgrimage of Jesus to the cross. The anguish in the garden where His disciples would not wait and watch with Him, falling asleep when He was facing the full force of the potential wrath. The arrest by a lynch mob that finds Him tried unjustly, whipped relentlessly and then sentenced without mercy. The long walk of shame to His death, made to physically carry, a cross, but spiritually carrying the shame of my sin. Then the final nail in the coffin is not the spike in His hand, the spear in his side or the slow death of asphyxiation, but rather the final spiritual separation from His Father turned judge: "God, why have you abandoned me?" Why? Because He is Holy! Holiness is played out by the Father, love played out by the Son, and the Spirit is waiting in the wings ready to be released once the penalty has been paid.

Perhaps some theologians will dislike the distinctive roles of the Trinity: the apparent family split, a scene that appears cruel to human understanding. But when we cast this picture against the backdrop of the awesome holiness of God we begin to dig into the depths of what was happening: perfect love was being expressed from perfect holiness. Western, twenty-first century mindsets need to press the reset button; we are too conditioned by our claustrophobic mindsets to understand the expanse of the scene. We need to have our minds spiritualised with heavenly reality, so that we see the human condition from the perspective of Heaven. Then we see the Father-Judge being true to His nature and the Son-Lover being true to His – a treaty for the sake of mankind is being played out; that which was far apart is being joined together. When the Holy Spirit is embraced and allowed to have full reign, we begin to get an understanding of the significance of the action of the cross. The penalty was paid, death was finally defeated and the full presence of God can cascade from Heaven to all who want it, desire it, seek it. Of course, Jesus promises it and now you can have it. Pentecost is the release of the heart of God to humanity. You know when the January sales are on and people queue outside designer shops to get a bargain? They wait all night in the cold to get that prized item, and then at 9.00am they rush into the store to clutch the bargain – the wait is over, their expectant prize is in reach. That is the Pentecost picture. The Holy Spirit is camped out ready to rush to claim the prize, or rather He is the prize ready to be captured by the punter! 9.00am comes and the disciples are all drunk with the heady mixture of the long anticipated presence of God – they have grasped the pearl of great price with both hands!

## Making light of holiness?

This chapter has been hard to write. Being a believer for 30 years I have embraced a grace message. Cut me in half and I ooze the grace of God. Yancey's book *What's So Amazing about Grace* cut me to the core, like many others at the time. I was fed in my formative years on a diet of grace, sitting under tutors of grace that sought to model it. I embraced renewal and cried genuine tears as I discovered that I was loved as a son by a Father. But something in me has shied away from the holiness message. Now, as I dig deeper into the love of God, as I sell out more to the call of God, I find myself unable to escape the allure of holiness. Holiness seems to be an inescapable part of the pearl that is beyond value.

# Endnotes

96. My paraphrase of Isaiah 6:1-10
97. 1 Samuel 2:2
98. See Acts 10:15
99. A. B. Davison
100. Psalm 71:22; 78:41; 89:18; Isaiah 1:4; 5:19,24
101. Isaiah 6:3; Revelation 4:8
102. Psalm 99:9; 99:3,5; 22:3
103. Isaiah 5:16
104. Exodus 20:5
105. Revelation 15:4
106. Isaiah 60:25
107. 1 Samuel 6:20
108. Hosea 9:9
109. Isaiah 67:15
110. Leviticus 11:44
111. Boice
112. 1 Peter 2:5
113. Exodus 20:11; Genesis 2:3
114. Psalm 127:2
115. Stanley Grenz

# People of Presence

I was brought up on the idea that salvation is a personal choice regarding a personal relationship with God. I had to know God "personally", as the little green Navigators book put it. When I was young the preachers would say, "Jesus would have died just for you – even if you were the only one to accept Him!" The Gospel was about personal faith; it was about the relationship that God wants with us; it is our choice to follow Him or not. I still believe this. I have a deep sense of the choice I have made to follow Christ. Jesus did call individuals to follow Him, and the message of salvation is still something that individuals need to accept. But I feel, however, that the individualism of the nineteenth and twentieth century Gospel message is inadequate for the age in which we live. When the reformers of the 16th Century rediscovered the idea of a personal faith they did so against the backdrop of a church culture which was overpowering; the corporate nature of Church was dominant and the individual subservient. Society today is torn between a desire to express the individual's personal freedom and the need to be in community. There is an uneasy tension that exists between personal liberty and the hunger for meaning in association with others. People still obviously have a deep ache for acceptance and recognition; we operate out of a desire to get noticed, be appreciated, be part of the gang. Take the phenomenal rise in online communities for example. Facebook allows users to be part of numerous communities, meaningful or superficial, without losing any personal freedom or power. In other words, we can belong but remain empowered as individuals.

Where does salvation fit into all of this? Is it a purely personal decision or is there a dimension to the Gospel message that makes the decision to come to Christ a corporate, community decision? It is interesting to see, thumbing through the book of Acts, that often decisions to accept the message of the Kingdom of God were not individual but community decisions. Perhaps a better way to put it is: whole communities of individuals committed themselves to follow Christ. At Pentecost, 3,000 people responded to the message at one time and more were added to the church on a daily basis. Crowds followed Peter after the healing of the beggar and soon the number of converts increased to "5,000 men" i.e. plus women and children. In this midst of this, we see individual conversions – the Ethiopian eunuch and Saul, soon to be known as Paul – but Cornelius got saved with a crowd and a jailor saw his family saved with him. In addition to this thought, all through the Bible we see God speaking frequently to communities of believers. I believe, therefore, that the norm should be a community response to the Gospel, rather than a series of individual ones. If I am right, it should affect and alter the way in which we attempt to reach people.

Whether or not we believe that the salvation message is for individuals or communities, we cannot refute the idea that God builds individuals into communities at conversion. The thread of God relating to us as a corporate body runs all the way through Scripture, from Abraham birthing a community, Moses leading a community, David ruling a community, Ezra and Nehemiah restoring the worth of a community, to Jesus discipling a community and now the explosion of New Testament communities that has multiplied ever since! God expresses Himself to and through a community of people.

As an aside, I am deeply concerned about the rise of the de-churched in our society: people who were once part of a church community who have now given up. I cannot help but think this must be a response either to weak or controlling leadership, the unreality of the community's expression of faith, or the desire to pursue "my own faith". I don't blame people. I have felt like giving up as well over the years. Sometimes it just seems too hard to make it work; it's too painful, too demanding. But then the pearl of great price demands a price – and that is the price of the Kingdom of God. If the presence of God, which is expressed through the community of God's people, is the pearl, then the price is your pride, your pain, your willingness to persevere. If you have opted out of the community of God's people, or are pursuing something on your own terms to satisfy your needs, can I implore you to rethink and reconnect with community? There is something about the presence of God that can only be expressed and felt through community.

## Holy people

Let's explore then what it means to be a "people of presence" – those who are corporately pursuing the pearl of great price. To my reckoning this involves two main ingredients: *holiness* and *unity*.

God spoke to Moses on Mount Sinai and said that His people, Israel, were to be "a kingdom of priests, a holy nation". In other words, a people who were able to mediate between God and man; a people who were to be set apart. God spoke this *before* He instituted the tabernacle worship, before He selected the Levites as the tribe of priests. Why? Because God wanted the whole of Abraham's seed to be a consecrated, a set-apart people described as holy because God is holy. Peterson writes that Israel, "as a holy nation, were to demonstrate what it means to live under the direct rule of God with God's sanctifying presence in their midst ... the Israelites were already a holy nation because God had drawn them to discover the awesome implications of being in such a relationship with Him ... [but] even a holy people could approach Him and relate to Him only in the terms that He laid down."

The biblical account tells us, however, that the response of the people to God was one of fear. They did not become that kingdom of priests because they did not go up the mountain when they should have done. So in order for God to fulfil some of His desire to dwell with man, in order to have that relationship, God decides to presence Himself in the tabernacle-temple-ark; to create a protected space where His holiness will not consume the ones He loves, but still allow Him to dwell in their midst, to live with them, go with them. The exiled prophet Ezekiel decrees the heart of God when he talks about the people of God returning from exile to the physical land of Israel:

*"I will display my holiness through you as all the nations will watch."*[116]

God is determined to display His nature through His people. The restoration and rescue of His people as HIS people is not only because He loves them, but because He is going to reveal His holiness in mankind, the very reason for the creation in the first place. Ezekiel goes on to prophesy,

*"I am bringing you back, but not because you deserve it. I am doing it to protect my holy name, on which you brought shame."*[117]

The very instruments that made God a global laughing-stock, that brought shame to His holy name, will be the paper on which He writes the final chapter of the story of His holiness. Cleansing and renewal is promised to the people of God. We will be given a new heart and a new spirit[118] – no more dirt to defile the holy presence of God – a complete wash and brush up so that we can stand in His presence. Jesus picks up this theme in His parable of the wedding banquet.[119] The normal invitees, the good and noble people, would not come to the banquet, so the invite is extended to the scruffy dog ends of society. As they came they were cleaned up and dressed appropriately for the wedding; the finery reserved for the holy ones was shared with the unholy. Washing and purity is a part of holiness!

## Unity

Ezekiel goes on to prophesy the reunification of the divided kingdoms of Israel and Judah.[120] You may remember that after Solomon, the nation of David was split into two when rival kings engaged in a power struggle. The consequence was the powerful kingdom was driven into disunity and what followed was years of kings deciding whether they would serve God or some idol! The nature of holiness must reflect the nature of a united God. We see unity demonstrated so perfectly in the oneness of the Godhead, three distinctive persons in one holy unified whole. Unity is essential for holiness. We will find it difficult to tread the highway of holiness without an active decision to operate in unity. Fractured relationships will cap, constrain and curtail the presence of God. I don't think we truly understand the destructive nature of disunity on the Body of Christ. How can we really expect the increased manifest presence of God to be displayed through our frail humanity unless we become pursuers of unity? If peace is the atmosphere of Heaven, then unity is the sun that shines. Peace will flow from unity.

Being involved in local church I get a first hand view of how unity affects people. Paul gave us some very practical teaching about how to live together in community. Offence, followed by anger, is the biggest destroyer of unity. Paul gives us straightforward advice, telling us very simply not to go to bed angry,[121] for instance. Anger may be a legitimate emotional response to someone or something, but the consequence is the potential for long term disunity and division. In Jesus' course, "An introduction to following Me" (otherwise called the Sermon on the Mount), the fourth lesson is on this subject.

*"If you are presenting a sacrifice at the altar in the temple and you suddenly remember that someone has something against you, leave your sacrifice there at the altar. Go and be reconciled to that person. Then come and offer your sacrifice to God"*[122]

His instructions are pretty clear. Can anyone tell me then, why believers in churches all over the world don't do this? When we hear of churches where people have not spoken to each other for decades, is it any wonder that the presence of God feels distant from the people of God? The story Jesus uses attacks the problem at the very point of someone being engaged in their act of worship. The person was bringing one of the Jewish sacrifices to the temple. If we are not reconciled with one another, then the inference of this passage is that our worshipping God is a complete waste of time. Notice that the onus of the responsibility is on us. It doesn't matter whether we are the offender or the offended. In Jesus' example the person offering the sacrifice is the offended party, who is encouraged to get it sorted straight away.

I am one of those people who can easily bring offence to others. It is part of my gift, but also part of my carnality. I have had to learn this lesson the hard way. Thankfully, I get emotionally paralysed if there are relationships in my life that are out of sorts. When I have been offended or offended someone else, I will go through my private rant on my own or with trusted people, speaking out my justifications for how I feel about the issue. Then, I soften, and it is not long before I have decided to say sorry for my part of the *contretemps*. Humbling ourselves is seldom easy, but always rewarding because we are cooperating with the Holy Spirit. We cannot be responsible for the reactions of others – they may never accept our protestations of apology. In fact, they may hold a grudge against us for the rest of their lives. But even if they do, at least, having apologised unreservedly, we can get back to the altar and get on with our sacrifice!

I am very serious when I point to this issue as being a major part of the reason why we do not see more of a move of the Holy Spirit in our communities. Holding onto anger and offence causes a hailstorm of bitterness and judgment that paralyses us. It wrecks our spiritual lives and the spiritual climate over our churches. "Anger" and its manipulative sister "gossip" cause such deep woundedness that we will never be trusted with the fullness of the manifest presence. A ripple of "share for prayer" can cause a wave of darkness that can plunge a community of God into decades of turmoil.

In the songs of ascent (Psalms 120-134) the pilgrims are journeying towards the holy place of God. They are on a holy pilgrimage to worship at the temple and meet with their God. The psalms take us nearer and nearer the temple, and as we reach the song that is sung in the temple, the penultimate song is a song for unity. Psalm 133 is an anthem to members of the community flowing in harmony and unity. My Bible (NLT) translates the word unity as "harmony", which I think is good. Good musicians flow together to create a harmony. Singers need to sing in tune, together, with each pitching the correct interval to achieve a sound of beauty, quality and excellence. Different instruments, each playing their part, but fitting together as a whole create a sound which is unified. Unity is not uniformity; unity is found in diverse expressions flowing together.

## How does unity work then?

Good question. The problem with institutional unity is that it is hard to make it work. The ecumenical movement has, for many years, attempted to do something structurally that has failed to deliver the very unity that is sought. Unity must be relationally based. True unity is fundamentally about unity of heart and purpose, of desire and behaviour. But relationships take time; they take investment and effort, and there are no quick fixes, no shortcuts.

As a church leader I have the dilemma of seeing the scriptural imperative of pursuing an agenda of unity and harmony, but never quite seeing the fruit of unity. Unity demands a high price; it costs us much. In fact, it is so costly that it demands dedicated determination to pursue. But structural or organisational unity can only flow from relational unity. There is a deeper dynamic that we are missing. Jesus was very clear about the issue of unity – a unity that reflected His unity with the Father. Fundamentally, we can only understand what true unity looks like as we grasp the relationship between the Father and the Son.

I'm still conflicted over the unity issue between churches. I know it is necessary; I know it is part of the package of pursuing the presence of God; yet it defies reason. It is elusive to the soulish man; it will only be grasped by our spirits. When I allow my Holy Spirit-infested spirit to dream and imagine, then I can see it. When I am led by the Spirit I can believe for a unity that will bust open the flood gates of Heaven and bring glory on earth. This is a unity that is much more than "getting along with each other"; it is definitely more than an organisational alliance or network; it can be attained only in the Spirit. If I commit to being presence led, then real unity is not far away! It's a pearl that is worth selling out for.

## Everyday unity

Let's put aside the inter-church variety of unity for a moment. What of unity and harmony in our daily lives? When we are caught in the middle of a militant juvenile strop it can seem as though there is anything but unity in our house! When our teenage daughter is moaning because we said no to a mid-week sleepover during term time ("You *always* say no!") ... when your son looks at you as like he is going to punch you ... where is the harmony of Heaven in these moments? We all face such challenges every day: stressful relatives, overbearing bosses, tantrum tots, unreasonable teens, manic drivers, rude shop assistants and worst of all ... computerised call centres! A counsellor would remind me at this point that anger is a choice, I can choose to be angry or not. Well it's too late telling me that now I'm too angry for words! Harmony in those times of frustration, anger and pain, is part of the great "secret" of the Gospel. Paul confidently asserts that he has learnt the secret of being content in all situations[123] – yeah right! (Of course, I know that he probably had learnt it, but remember this is an older, experienced man giving us his sage reflections on life). In his very next letter, Paul shows us a prayer that will help us achieve it and live "productive" lives which produce heavenly fruit.[124] The answer? Knowledge of God's will and spiritual understanding is the key to rising above the stuff of life and being fruitful. When the muck is flying, the ability to rise above it is what we must crave for normal everyday harmony. This is what hanging out in the presence of God begins to give us, the more we do it: *a heavenly perspective of earthly stuff.* When we know God, know His will for our lives, our planet, when we start to think like the spiritual beings that we are, then perhaps we can rise above our "momentary troubles"[125] and attain that glory.

I write this when a dear friend is sick with cancer. We are praying for a full recovery and believing God, but when the chips are down and we can no longer rely on frail human wisdom, or when the best strategy of man is spent, then actually we would be wise to have learnt this lesson. To get divine wisdom requires a huge act of surrender; it requires a massive leap of faith and at times you just wonder what the heck you are doing with your life! I have another friend who has pretty much been wrecked by God for anything other that praying! God has got on his case so much that my friend knows he must do nothing else but pursue this costly life, a yielded life of prayer.

To attain the sublime lofty heights of spiritual understanding takes time, perseverance, tears, and frustrated shouts at God – but it is in this pursuit that the secrets of the Gospel of harmony are found.

## Holiness : declared, designed, destined

God is pretty clear with us in Scripture about the need for us to be holy: *"You must be holy because I am holy"*[126] – okay God, I think I get the message. Thankfully, the secret of the Gospel is that He doesn't leave us to our own devices. Ezekiel declares that God's holiness will be revealed through His people, the covenant between God and man is restored, the Davidic kingdom re-established and the temple rebuilt for evermore[127], whoopee! Eugene Peterson puts it like this: "the paradox of holiness is that God acts to judge everything that is unholy and yet provides a way of cleansing and sanctification for sinners ... God's offspring would be holy because of His actions on their behalf." I can't tell you what a relief this is. We are not holy because we try our hardest to live holy lives; we are holy because God says we are! When God speaks about the priesthood in the Old Testament, He declares them holy because He says they are.[128] Paul, the great biblical theologian, takes up this theme using the analogy of bread dough. When a portion of it is submitted as an offering it is holy, so it makes the whole batch of dough holy. Or the tree analogy: if the roots are holy, then the whole tree is holy. Thank God we get grafted on to this holy tree![129] God likes to address us by our heavenly status rather than our physical reality. He operates in faith, the very thing we are supposed to operate in!

We are not only declared holy by God,[130] but we are designed to be holy. R.T. Kendall says that holiness, "is what He wants us to be", or, as Paul says, *"put on the new self, created to be like God in true righteousness and holiness."*[131] Holiness is part of our divinely created nature. Adam was created holy; it is in the very nature of man to be holy; we have spirits so that we can encapsulate the essence of holiness, so we don't need to buy into the lie of the devil that we can never be holy. God has declared that we are holy and we are designed to be holy. In fact, Paul goes even further by saying that God actually had us in mind as holy beings long before creation[132]... now that is a bit mind blasting, it messes me up to think that God had my holiness in mind!

But why is it then that I do stuff that is anything but holy, in fact I seem to spend my life searching for holiness? We need to see our life with eyes of faith. God ordained us to be holy, and God has said that we are, so now we must operate in it. Or, as Peter puts it, *"he who called you is holy, so be holy in all you do."*[133] Okay then! There is a huge call to the Body of Christ to be holy, that's why in any move of God's presence holiness becomes a big deal. The God who determines that we are holy wants us to start acting like we are holy. We are not called to live a sinful, impure life, but a holy one[134] – a life connected to the reality of heaven, a heaven-focussed and heaven-centred life, a life that takes on the character of God. Does it mean that it will all just happen? No. We may have moments of encounter, where the unholy in us gets stripped away and we walk away very different. I have heard the stories of people who were once druggies or bound up in some other way, in a moment get delivered from their addiction. Holiness can happen in a moment of encounter as Isaiah proves when the burning coals hits his lips.[135] But this is not the norm. Most of us have to work it out in our lives. We may get an encounter to kick start the sanctification process, but in the main we are supposed to sort it out as we go along. Eugene Peterson says, "consecration as a human response is made possible by God's initiative through His Son, cleansing people and consecrating them to Himself for eternity". Holiness is not our idea, but nevertheless we have to do something about living holy lives.

## Jesus: Jedi Master of holiness

Being a Star Wars fan (I wonder if they will ever make episode 7, but don't go to Star Wars conventions at weekends, just to clarify) I love the concept of the Jedi Masters. They sit in the Jedi Counsel weighing matters of spiritual importance, are dedicated to the Jedi order of living, and then seek to implement that order through their universal policing duties. Jesus must be the Jedi master of holiness. He knows His stuff when it comes to holy living. Jesus is our holiness – we are not holy because of our own endeavours, but holy because of Him. He makes us holy, identifies us with His family which has holiness as its very nature, and gives us the ability to live a holy life through His power. Jesus prayed for us that we would be made holy by God's truth,[136] then in the very next verse He offers Himself as a holy sacrifice, so we can be made holy by God's

truth. This is wisdom and action all rolled into one. Listen to
the apostles' take on this truth:

*"It is because of him that you are in Christ Jesus, who has
become for us wisdom from God—that is, our righteousness, holiness
and redemption ... But now he has reconciled you by Christ's physical
body through death to present you holy in his sight, without blemish
and free from accusation ... we have been made holy through the
sacrifice of the body of Jesus Christ once for all ... he who has saved
us and called us to a holy life—not because of anything we have
done but because of his own purpose and grace. This grace was
given us in Christ Jesus before the beginning of time, but it has
now been revealed through the appearing of our Saviour, Christ
Jesus, who has destroyed death and has brought life and immortality
to light through the gospel."*[137]

We are only able to be called "holy" because the Master
enabled us to be called holy. I find that these passages take the
pressure off me. I realise that if I get into a place of trying too
hard and failing to be a holy man, I have not lost the reality of
my holiness. Holiness is the gift of God. The way we decide to
live and the choices we make are a reflection of how much we
work that gift out in our lives. The Pearl Hunter story shines a
light on a man who finds the thing he desires most and goes
after it with everything he has. Holiness is part of that pearl,
that gift.

As believers, God does not force us to live a holy life. We can
bottle out and settle for a life less full on, a life of complacency
and compromise. We may say to God, "Thanks for the offer of
fullness of life, but I rather like my sexual partner, my standard
of living and my overindulgence. I'll do my Sunday duty and
pay my dues, but don't make too many demands on me. It
doesn't fit my way of life at the moment." Pearl Hunters, however, have grasped the importance and meaning of pursuit
because they have tasted something that cannot be assuaged by

compromise. Pearl Hunters will never be satisfied with the last experience they had of God – they will always want more – the pursuit of the ultimate.

## The quest for holy living

To me, the quest for holiness is part and parcel of the pursuit of the priceless treasure. I know I cannot get there on my own, it is only as I am found in Christ that I will realise the potential of holiness. But I also know that to experience the fullest expression of Heaven on earth, I need to be advancing towards the prize of personal holiness. It is a lifestyle that yields incalculable rewards.

Holiness is our destination. It has to be, since Heaven is where we are headed and holiness pervades its atmosphere. But holiness is a journey, a quest to be taken seriously.[138] Paul recognised that there is a struggle for holiness, a struggle to reach our endgame, the object of our affection, the essential truth. Paul entreated the Roman church to pursue a "slave life" committed to holiness. In other words, to get radical about living right.

We are so used to being slaves to sinful desire, with sin crouching at our door ready to entice us to some shady end. Proverbs tells the story of young men being pounced on by well endowed, bored housewives, who want to lure them off to bed while hubby is out of town! That is so like sin, to lurk around and then POUNCE! Sin enslaves, but Paul implores us to be enslaved by the order of holiness, to make it our priority to live holy lives.

Peterson has wisdom here. Believers are "sanctified or made holy by God's manifesting Himself to them, drawing them into a special relationship with Himself and making provision for their sinfulness ... they are called to live in a way that demonstrates the reality of their relationship with God and with one another." Holiness is the best way to relate to each other, a way devoid of jealousy and self-interest. In a holy life there is no hidden angst, no unspoken agenda, no resentment stored away for another day. A holy life is transparent, yielded, confident, generous. It is something amazing to attain. Ultimately, holiness is the password that allows us to ascend the hill of the Lord, to enjoy His presence in its fullness, to experience divine paradise.[139] In holy living we get the key to the door to experience to the fullest extent the reality of Heaven on earth. Our *status* before God is that of holiness, so we can come into His presence any time we like, but our quest is also the *physical* expression of holiness: a decision made on the inside that we are determined to live aligned to our status.

Holiness is part of our discipline as believers. God is disciplining us to be holy so that we may share in His holiness.[140] If we hope to grasp the full nature of the holiness that has been bought by Jesus, then we need to allow the discipline of holiness to come upon us. We commit ourselves to a life of pursuing holiness[141] and in the process, love becomes intertwined with holiness. The stereotypical sour faced puritan preacher is a parody of holiness, because the inevitable consequence of holiness is an expression of genuine love. Finger wagging legalism has nothing to do with genuine holiness; where is the love in that?

## Holiness our end goal

The ultimate destiny of the Church is that Jesus presents to Father a "holy" Church, one whose character is like God's, with no stains, no wrinkly bits, no bits swept under the carpet – a spotless Bride.[142] The end time "sound" will be that of a holy God coming back to take His bride. That's why the book of Revelation tells of a holy Judge of all, finally sorting everything out and bringing His permanent holiness to Earth. There is a great picture of the presence of God finally resting on earth at the end of the prophecy of Zechariah.[143] Everything gets the title "holy", even the harness bells on the horses and the kitchenware! That's it, the final picture of a glorious future where everything gets the name "holy". Holiness will eventually be the culture of Heaven and Earth. It will be the way stuff gets done in the future government. Well, that has got to be worth hunting out, hasn't it?

## Endnotes

116. Ezekiel 20:41
117. Ezekiel 36:22
118. Ezekiel 36:25-27
119. Matthew 22:1-14
120. Ezekiel 37:22-24
121. Ephesians 4:26
122. Matthew 5:23-24
123. Philippians 4:11
124. Colossians 1:9-10
125. 2 Corinthians 4:17
126. Leviticus 19:2
127. Ezekiel 37:26-28
128. Leviticus 21:7-8
129. Romans 11:16
130. Colossians 3:12
131. Ephesians 4:24
132. Ephesians 1:4
133. 1 Peter 1:15
134. 1 Thessalonians 4:7
135. Isaiah 6
136. John 17:17
137. 2 Timothy 1:9-10
138. Romans 6:19,22
139. Psalm 24:3
140. Hebrews 12:10
141. Hebrews 12:14
142. Ephesians 5:27
143. Zechariah 14:20-21

# Pursuit

As part of our church Easter celebrations we decided to hold an all night prayer and worship time in our building. Some of our younger guys organised this, so there was lots of energy and edgy expressions of worship. I decided to come down and hang out in the prayer sanctuary between midnight and 3.00am. So Macbook in hand, a few of my favourite study Bibles, and a couple of commentaries (just to impress the young people that I am deeply learned man) I found a comfortable spot and started to pray. The musicians on stage played an improvised set which included a mix of sung worship and Bible reading. The music was great, in fact more than great, and it lifted me. Then suddenly I "saw" or sensed something, not in my natural eyes but in the Spirit. I can't say I saw a picture or anything, but my memory of the event is left with an overwhelming sense of this "impression".

## Incensed!

In Revelation we read of an angel mixing the physical incense from the temple incense burner with prayers that have somehow been collected from the saints of God (that's you and me) on Earth. They are blended into a fireball that becomes the fuel of the judgement that explodes from Heaven. Powerful stuff![144]

Earlier in Revelation, the elders (a select, representative group of authority figures on Earth) held golden bowls full of incense which are also described as the "prayers of the saints"[145] and the waft of these smoking prayers are accompanied by singing. It is a graphic portrayal of the heavenly scene – our heartfelt prayers becoming spiritual incense. David sang a song to God where he compared his prayer to incense.[146] What an evocative idea, God in Heaven "smelling" our prayer life. He literally smells the aroma of our hearts, like a roast dinner cooking in the oven, the smell of His people fills Heaven with fragrance and whets the divine appetite. Is it any wonder then that one of Jesus' birthday presents was frankincense, a vital ingredient of incense? Jesus was going to be the best example of prayer ever – One whose very destiny was to intercede for humanity.

This is what I caught a glimpse of on that Easter night as I sat with our amazing, passionate twenty-somethings, worshipping while holding down the night watch. I smelled the aroma (not physically, but in the Spirit) of our prayers being like incense. The experience was so real and tangible that it caused me to go on a scriptural search for the meaning of incense. To my surprise, despite their being 145 references to incense in Scripture, there was little to be found in my dictionaries and commentaries. In fact, there does not appear to be any explicit reason given why there was an incense burner before the Lord in the Holy of Holies (Exodus 30), it was just there because God directed it to be there! This was like a red rag to a bull: I wanted to know why! One brilliant, though heavy going, commentary by Kiel-Dietz says the holy of holies is the place where we have been made right with God, so the altar of incense is where the prayers of those who have been made righteous go up, so they can be heard by God. The altar in the outer court-yard of the temple is all about the redemption of man, the sorting out of the sin problem (as the Message Bible puts it), where the

Hebrews sacrificed their offerings to make themselves acceptable before God. These sacrifices made a way for man's representative (the priest) to enter the secret place, the holy place.

So God makes us holy, despite the fact we don't deserve it, and when it comes to the altar burning in the holy of holies, we are already made right with God and our prayers have access to Him and can change stuff in the Heavenlies and on Earth. If you believe the graphic portrayal of prayer in Revelation, it is our prayers that will cause a judgement to come on earth! If that is a bit too heavy for you, then at least believe that *"the earnest prayer of a righteous person has great power and produces wonderful results."*[147] This is a pretty convincing argument for prayer! The high priest was commanded to check the incense regularly, twice a day, so to take a spiritual reality from this physical symbol, we conclude it is our duty, no our desire, to burn incense to God, to pray, to worship, to occupy His presence with our presence.

## Pray continually

The psalmist talks about praying "night and day"[148], a favourite verse of House's of Prayer everywhere. Sitting in the aroma of the presence that night, I got a glimpse of what Paul meant when he said things like "pray continually"[149] and "we have not stopped praying for you".[150] As the air of the auditorium filled with spiritual incense, I felt the command of God to set up our own house of prayer. I am still not sure about my New Testament theology for such a venture, but if God says to do it, I better get on with it. It is not like others are not doing the same thing. Houses of Prayer are springing up all over the world. The organic global prayer movement, 24-7 Prayer are birthing prayer houses, prayer rooms and capturing the imagination of a previously prayerless Church.[151] IHOP in Kansas has been conducting continuous day and night prayer for over ten years, using their "harp and bowl" model.[152] Our meagre efforts have made me realise just how bankrupt we as a church had become in our prayer life, yet one of the prime objectives of the church is to pray? Doh!

Historically, one of the dullest and most sparsely attended meetings in the church calendar has been the prayer meeting. Why? Possibly because we have made it the dullest meeting there is, but that is really not good enough. No revival that I have ever come across has ever started without a prayer movement. Reading recently about the Moravian prayer movement that started at Herrnhut in Germany has made me see the connections again between mission – prayer – presence. We are not called just to mission or just to enjoy God's presence. We are called to pray, which in turn fuels both our experience of the presence and our expression of mission. And prayer is not something for the specialist intercessors to engage in – it is something we are all to do. Like many, I am still not a very good pray-er – it's a work in progress – but God is drawing our hearts so that we can dig into Him more and more.

Jesus stood in the temple and was filled with a holy anger by the commercialisation of holiness. Trading and money making had reduced the centrepiece of the presence of His Father into a den of robbers. Jesus declared, *"My temple will be called a house of prayer for all nations"*[153] and it was anything but that. He wanted it restored to its true purpose. One of the exile prophets, Amos, prophesied about the restoration of the *"fallen tent of David."*[154] The fulfilment of that could, of course, point to Jesus, but as with so much biblical prophecy it speaks to us on many levels and across many generations. Looking around the Church I see a restoration of true Davidic worship in progress, though it is by no means complete or full. My colleague and friend, Paul Miche, who directs our worship says,

"It is true that we are all temples of the Holy Spirit and that God has called us to pray individually. But it would probably be true to say that most of us don't prioritise this area in our lives, and the role and significance of prayer is not what God intended. A physical space given over to prayer is a tangible way of saying that we are making room for this, whatever the cost. We are saying of the physical space that of all the activities that take place inside this building, prayer ought to be at the top of the list! It is an opportunity to make space in our lives and give ourselves to Him. God is looking to bring Heaven and Earth together through fellowship with His bride (see Ephesians 1:10). The Prayer House would also be an opportunity for God to establish a place of rule, advancing His Kingdom and dominion in a tangible way."

As a local church we have valued the presence of God in a very visible way. We put a high priority on worship and are known for our worship. As we have shifted some of our thinking, we are exploring the idea that perpetual and consistent worship is the "engine room" of our Kingdom activity. The ship (church) is a missional entity on course for a God-given desti-nation, so worship and prayer are the engine room that fuels and powers the ship. However, to continue the maritime illustration, too much of our worship is like the palm court orchestra on the sun deck – just there to entertain the fare-pay-ing passengers!

Making the church a house of prayer is about fuelling our mission. We become fruitful if we are attached to the vine.[155] Being fruitful in all we do flows out of our deeper intimacy with God. When we "stand in the courts of God" and praise [156] we are giving God something. Too much of our so-called worship is about a feel good factor, rather than offering something to God. Very often our emphasis is trying to get something from God, rather than giving Him something. The nature of God is giving, but that is not the reason we worship! Engine room praying is hidden, not glitzy. Like an old steam ship, the engine room team are tough men, shovelling coal into hot fires – there is nothing glamorous about this sort of praying. When I think of a house of prayer, I am thinking of something that involves hard work, effort and determination, something that keeps us going. Has church lost its propulsion because it has stopped being fuelled by constant prayer and worship? I wonder whether the monastic traditions had the right idea. For centuries they were up early praying and continued through the day, giving themselves to the pursuit of God. Sure the monks, like just about every other movement, lost their way, but the heartbeat of a people in hot pursuit of God was foundational to their order.

When I was sitting at 2.00am, listening to the worship band serenade God, a key verse jumped out at me that referred to the burning of incense by the newly instituted priesthood. God tells Moses that, *"this must be done from generation to generation."*[157] In other words, they were to pass on the priestly task of burning incense to God from one generation to the next. The Church today is full of priests; we have the priesthood of all believers and there is something completely awesome about the responsibility to keep our prayers alive before God, to keep the aroma of a passionate people burning before His throne. If that alone isn't justification for houses of prayer all over our nation, I don't know what is!

## Pilgrimage

My momentary glimpse of prayers rising as incense has set me on a quest to understand this spiritual connection between Heaven and Earth, though I feel completely inadequate for the task of understanding this lofty calling. My Charismatic Evangelical theology tends to reduce my experience of the presence of God to my baptism of the Holy Spirit – the correct idea that I have been filled with the Holy Spirit of God and so now contain His presence. But my spirit is crying out to me, "Don't stop there!" Why do we limit our experience of the Holy Spirit to what we can carry about within us? I have had a glimpse of Heaven and like all peeks behind the invisible curtain, you get trapped by a desire to experience more. Yes, I have seen the pearl of great price and now I am a pearl hunter.

Pursuit is seen in the biblical concept of pilgrimage. On a pilgrimage we set out to seek something greater, something lofty, something divine. The modern believer will trek to Florida, Toronto, California, Kansas, Seoul, in fact any place where something spiritual is happening. Why? Is it only about consumerist spirituality or is there a deep desire that has been awakened? A heart fixated with an impression of divine grace, a heart that wants to pursue the experience of heavenly reality, a heart that has seen something of such value, will actively seek out the divine.

## Songs that take us higher

The Psalms of Ascent[158] track the journey of pilgrim worshippers on their way to the great temple. They are songs that display so openly the frailty and purpose of the Jewish worshipper, going on their pilgrimage, and they impart great lessons to contemporary pursuers of the presence. What I love about these Psalms are the themes that recur as they travel on the journey, themes of devotion and humanity. We can be tempted to believe that the pursuit of God is reserved only for the pious or devout, those holy enough to make time and space for the journey. But my experience of the journey to God's presence is not at all pious, rather it is a desperate attempt to get something of reality! My own journey to "find" God in a deeper way has mostly been motivated by a need for breakthrough and a new start. God is good at giving people fresh starts and "rebirth" is His speciality.

We see in these psalms, as the pilgrims get closer and closer to the temple, that they relinquish more and more of their personal baggage – the worry, cares or anger that beset them – and embrace the holiness of their destination. I offer below a somewhat colloquial impression of these psalms. For me they capture the essence of pursuit, of trying to find heaven in the fuzz of life. Don't therefore look at the paragraphs below as a serious academic translation, they are not, but for me the journey into the heart of God is an experience full of frustration, anger and eventual submission to the higher power we love and serve! If I was a poet I would have written this in verse, but as the poetic touch has eluded me I will stick to what I know I can do. You may like to read the psalm as my personal reflection, tinged with real life sentiment. They crescendo towards the climax when the psalmist is in the physical place of the presence of God – the final destination of the pilgrimage.

### Song 120: Trouble

"Ah! They are all out to get me God. In fact, I am sick to the back teeth of the cretinous people that I work and live with. If you don't get me out of this mess, I don't know what I'll do. The things they have said about me are so untrue, it is like being spiked by needles, I am completely worn out God! I need to find peace. I'm on a quest for inner peace, peace with myself, peace with others, peace with God. Despite the fact that I can't hear peace in my life right now, that is want I want."

### Song 121: Attentive!

"I'm not going to find any peace through the solutions offered up by retail therapy. No, I need to go to a higher power to find peace; that's where I will get help! I'm going to the Eternal Architect to get peace for my troubled soul. He is always alert, attentive to my distress, that's the help I need. God is not having a kip on the sofa, He is always looking, always watching, always on guard. Finally, someone that is really interested in me, someone who is going to take the brunt of the trouble, someone who is on my side. I'm on my journey into the Protector!

## Song 122: Justice

"My friend came to me and said that they were making the journey to the "House of God". Frankly, I couldn't say, "Yes, I'll come!" quickly enough. That's what I need to get out of this messy situation: a journey to God. It's an amazing feeling standing in the place where God lives. I feel safe even as it's just coming into view. This is the place where I will get the justice that I deserve, where God Almighty will come to my defence. Suddenly, I feel at peace. Something about the place where God is brings me peace for my life, the place of justice is the place of peace. Not just peace, but also a sense of wellbeing, a place where life is good."

## Song 123: Attentive!

"Now my eyes are on Him, no longer on my problems. Sitting in this place takes me away from the raging strife that I live in. I find myself at home ... He's got my attention! I am hanging on His every move like a waiter being attentive to his diner. I'm in a place where I am attentive to Him. Really, I have had my fill of life my way; its time to look to you God!"

## Song 124: Testimony

"Just reflecting for a minute, there have been many times when God has been on my side. In fact, I wonder what it would be like if God had not been there for me? He has bailed me out of trouble so many times. Remembering how God has come to the rescue before, why wouldn't He come to the rescue again? He is powerful, as my own journey proves. My help is from the great Creator God. He has got creation all worked out, so He can work out my minor problems."

### Song 125: Surrounded

"The safest place I know is the place called "Trust God". There is no doubt that when all else fails, when evil seems to be crouching at my every move, when I feel surrounded by trouble at every side, actually God has already surrounded me. He brings me the safety of the walled city, He makes it my safe place. God, don't let bad men take government of the land. Stop those who have their hearts set on the wrong things from having free reign. Let good men rule."

### Song 126: Restoration

"It's like a daydream come true! We are home again where we belong, back to the promised place, God has brought revival and restoration to His people – the celebration has started. After all that grief, we need to let our hair down and party! That's so like God: He turns making something out of nothing into an art form. The desolate industrial wastelands are now new, state of the art gleaming developments. It's what He does – the God of the turnaround, of restoration, of renewal. We can spend our lives crying over our troubles and hardships, but when God the Harvester comes, the tears spent earlier in our lives will reap happy songs of abundance. It's so like Him."

### Song 127: Builder

"I've discovered this truth: you have got to build something by the maker's instructions or it will never get built at all. It's true you know, there are no short cuts, build it by the Architect's design! Human effort is a complete waste of time unless we get the heart of God. Being a workaholic can't satisfy the needs of the inner-man. In fact, being any kind of "holic" is only going to leave you deeply craving something more. The reward of the satisfied is rest, but don't think that by being a lazy slob you are going to get satisfied – that will inevitably lead somewhere else! I've discovered this truth as well: the true nature of blessing is seeing our kids grow up healthy and whole. I think the only reward I really want is seeing my natural and spiritual children grow to fulfil their potential. You can achieve much with young men and women – shoot them out against injustice, to shape a nation, to change lives. When we live in a thriving community of young people we cannot be ashamed or accused. This is true building – investing in the lives of the next generation.

## Song 128: Prosperity

"Prosperity in a material consumer world is not a matter of possessions. The truth is it is so much more than stuff. You want joy? Well learn to reverence God and obey Him. Not a very modern concept, I know, but that is where you will find true happiness. It is obvious to work and get a reward in terms of remuneration, but that is really not the be all and end all of life. True blessing is having a wife that feels she is fruitful in all her endeavours, emotionally free and happy. True blessing is to sit round the Christmas meal table, laughing and messing with your children, their spouses and your grandkids. Sitting at the head of my table, engaged in the banter, I can sit back in my armchair and say, "I am truly blessed."

## Song 129: Scars

"I could be defined by my history, my mistakes and the abuses of life. I can contemplate the way in which I have had a tough life and let that define my emotions and character. But I am not going to be defeated by the hand that life has dealt me, whether or not it is my fault. No matter how scarred my back gets, I am wearing those scars as badges of honour. My past does not have to define my future. The ropes that have tied me down will just fray and snap. Those who come against me (human or spirit) will just wither away, defeated!

### Song 130: Forgiveness

"God, I have completely messed up. After all my confident, faith-filled assertions I am a bit of a mess. If I was to be judged by my mistakes then I am completely stuffed. I am crying out now from a place of emptiness. I have nothing to give, thank you God that you forgive without holding back. You keep forgiving because it is Your nature. I am pretty sober now, I really do have to completely depend on you God. You have to come through for me. Now I'm hanging on, waiting ... waiting... waiting. I have realised another truth in this journey: the love of God goes on and on, never tripping up, never missing a beat. I live in the continual overflow of God's love. Being redeemed is not a quick fix, it takes time; it takes a lifetime."

### Song 131: Still

"I'm nearing the end of my journey. Feeling forgiven, I can say that all the angst is gone from me now. I feel pretty humbled in Your presence. Somehow, being low before You means that your way, which is the better way, can be released. Why do I try to concern my little brain with lofty ideas? Dumb really. If I just trusted in You, I would be content. I am not going to cry out and be all angry with you. No, I will still myself and in that stillness find contentment."

## Song 132: Presence

"I'm nearer still the presence of God. The story of your desire to presence Yourself with us, mere man, is an amazing one. David, the man whose heart was full of desire for you, desperately wanted to restore the Ark of your Covenant to the place where it belonged, in Holy Jerusalem. David was consumed with this passion. God, I want to be consumed by that passion too. He vowed to return the presence of God to the centre of God's community. That's my vow, Lord God. Your presence will be at the centre of my life and I want it back at the centre of Your people. The presence is not something that can be messed around with. Poor old Uzzah only tried to stop the Ark falling over and he got zapped! But lending You a hand is not necessary unless You ask us for our hands. Holiness is not a light issue. I don't want to confuse grace with liberty or love with license. No, it is time to approach God as Sovereign. Of course He is Father ... Daddy ... but right now in my pilgrimage, God is God, sitting on His throne administering justice. His power is total and everywhere He is, there is peace. God, I need to be clean, need to be right before You, need to be washed. It's your rule, King Jesus, that I seek. You are sitting on David's throne over the Kingdoms of this earth. You have made Your resting place on Earth with mankind. When Your presence is among us, then stuff happens. Prosperity flows from Your presence, cities prosper, poverty is alleviated, priests become holy, songs are sung, rulers exercise just power, leaders lead right and enemies turn back in shame. Bring on the presence of God.

## Song 133: Unity

"I'm very close. I'm one step away. Harmony amongst friends and brothers is essential in the place of the presence of God. I can't be out of sorts with my brothers, otherwise I am out of sorts with God. God links our relationships with each other to our relationship with Him. This is the last song I will sing until I sing in the holy place. Harmony is precious to You. It is like oil used in anointing: the depth of the unity will saturate the very fabric of our lives. God can see our attempts to live at peace with our brothers, we can't deceive Him. Harmony with each other will soften us, it makes us more receptive to You Lord. When we are at peace with one another we can receive so much more from You. When we live in the place of harmony, You take it upon Yourself to command a blessing. God commands blessing and when He commands it, it jolly well gets done.

### Song 134: Holy

"Oh, my goodness ... I've made it to the place of God. My pilgrimage is at an end. I have arrived at the top step of the temple and all I can do is erupt in praise to my God. This is the place of constant praise with servants of God dedicated to worshipping Him day and night. This is the place of eternal and ceaseless praise to God. I hold my hands up in surrender, supplication, openness, yieldedness, in praise to God. I am face to face with the Creator of the Universe. Let God bless you! No more words seem appropriate in the presence of God, so ... enough said."

### Presence is where God is

At the end of this mini-pilgrimage we arrive at the very temple of God. John described Jesus as dwelling with us. The word "dwelling" means "tabernacled" [159] – Jesus was the permanent presence of the divinity. Revelation tells us that *"the **dwelling** of God is with men, and he will live with them."* [160] There is a view that has gathered some credibility and resonance with churches that the weekly gathering of the saints is not that important or is only to be seen as an evangelistic opportunity. I think we have lost the reason for meeting on a Sunday. True church is only understood in a holistic sense. It is about a whole life experience. The relationships we build, the way we live out our lives at work, our gathering in meaningful groups – this is church. So why do we emphasise the collective worship gathering, normally on a Sunday morning? I am convinced that the gathering of "church" makes a collective gateway to Heaven, a contact place for God to meet with His people. Is God really finished with any concept of the temple? Does God no longer value a physical place on Earth? Of course God wants to meet with the individual (Evangelical teaching has made sure that we know God personally), but what about that the divine corporation (the Trinity of God) meeting with the corporate Body of Christ on Earth? Our collective worship and gatherings should be occasions where His subjects seek an audience with the King of kings, where the Father meets His sons. Our passion should be the cry of Moses: "Show us your glory!"

We, like the tabernacle, should be portable, responsive to the desires of God. When He speaks, we say "yes", responding to His every command. If your church structure is too cumbersome, too awkward, then dismantle it and rebuild it so that finally the organisation of the church can serve the vision and mandate of Jesus Christ. Tear down that which is not of God and build the spiritual entity that God wants. Don't be fooled into minimising church to some social club, where collective worship is an occasional pastime, a remembrance of a yesteryear. I don't think this needs to be on Sunday, nor do I think it needs to be large, but it is an intentional means of corporately accessing the presence of God and hearing Him speak collectively to His people.

The mandate of Scripture is clear to me. We are to pursue God in pilgrimage, but more than that, we are to pursue Him together. We may fear losing our identity in the corporate malaise that sometimes passes for "church", but the truth is: it is when we seek God together that we really find Him. And in that setting, God speaks to us about His desires and purposes for His collective people. As we seek God, wholeheartedly together, then we will be truly distinctive.

## Endnotes

144. Revelation 8:3-5
145. Revelation 5:8
146. Psalm 141:2
147. James 5:16
148. Psalm 134:1
149. 1 Thessalonians 5:17
150. Colossians 1:9
151. www.24-7prayer.com
152. www.ihop.com
153. Mark 11:17
154. Amos 9:11
155. John 15
156. Psalm 134,135
157. Exodus 30:8
158. Psalms 120-134
159. John 1:14
160. Revelation 21:3

# Deeper

## Divine encounters

Isaiah's experience of God was pretty astounding. As he witnessed an amazing vision of the very throne room of God, he was completely undone. It was a life-changing moment, a full on confrontation with the Living God. In a moment where spiritual reality invaded human reality, Isaiah' life was transformed for good. From then on he was a man on a mission, a man with a message. Here is my take on the amazing scene unfolded in Isaiah chapter 6:

> *The nation was in transition, the future looked uncertain, and the young prophet was seeking the will of the "Holy One". He had questions about his future, questions about the nation. He had a heart cry. Suddenly, he found himself in a different place, he was having one of his visions, a vision of something lofty, something other worldly. He saw the Holy One sitting on the throne of Heaven. He had been transported to the place where the God of all rules the physical and spiritual realms. This was a gob smacking experience. He had had visions before, but never of this magnitude, never with such vivid colours and smells. This was a Technicolor, multi-sensory spiritual experience like he had never experienced before! The*

*God of glory was sitting on His throne, His royal robe of majesty was so incredible it filled the entire room. It seemed as if the King of kings was arrayed in full coronation gear. The King had winged angelic attendants; no childlike cutesy cherubs, these were mighty muscular angelic beings who effortlessly served the King.*

*The angel's faces were covered with their wings out of reverence and submission to the Supreme Commander of the Heavenly forces. It was as if the brightness of the Lord was more than they could bear; it was like they were looking into the sun and being blinded by the light, their wings protecting their eyes from the burning rays. As they hovered around the presence of God, they had two other wings covering their feet, as though it would be irreverent to allow their feet to touch the ground near to the throne. With a third pair of wings they hovered around the throne shouting out to each other, "Holy, holy, holy". It was more than a declaration of fact – it was a salute, a shout of honour, a royal title. This trinity of sound seemed to be the only thing appropriate to be expressed at this moment; it was the "correct" shout, a statement summing up the moment. "Holy, holy, holy is the Commander-in-Chief of all the Heavenly armies!" In other words, the Supreme Warrior was "set apart", different, and with a nature above and beyond any other being. "Earth is filled with His glory," the angels continued, expressing how the physical realm occupied by the young prophet was completely surrounded and endued the with nature of God. Not "will be" filled, but simply "filled". At that moment, according to "Heaven time", Earth was not the confused, sin-infested realm that the prophet experienced – it was the cradle of glory!*

*These words of prophetic declaration, "Holy, holy, holy," shook the sanctuary of the heavenly palace like an earthquake, yet the throne room didn't fall down. Smoke filled the room as though it was on fire. It was overwhelming; it was beyond understanding. The prophet could not stand the awesome scene any more. He screamed, as if it was his last breath, "It's over!" The prophet had glimpsed his sinfulness in that moment as the holiness of the scene crashed into the dirt of his mortality. The wreckage of his emotions was confusion, devastation, a deep knowing of his sinful state next to the white majesty of God. So why wasn't he brushed aside with a fiery breath? Why was he still alive? Surely the stain of his life could not remain in the presence of God?*

*One of the mighty attendants came towards the young prophet with a burning coal from the altar. The coal was bright and hot, burning with the glory of God. Black coal from the mines on Earth had been so infused with glory that it shone brightly; something dark and hard had been transformed into a container of the glory. So it was possible, darkness could be changed into a light carrier. The hot coal flew at the prophet and hit his mouth. The prophet now became the very carrier of light and glory, just as the coal had been, in an instantaneous transferral of power. The King's servant decreed, "You are no longer guilty, you are forgiven." Redemption and acceptance now flowed into the prophet, prostrate on the floor. The darkness and heaviness that had confronted him only a moment ago had vanished. This was a new start, a wiping of the slate!*

*Then the King addressed the gathered courtiers: "I need to send a message to the people on Earth. Who can I entrust with this message?" Before he could reflect on these words, a holy enthusiasm surged through the prophet and he found himself volunteering to be the message carrier. With new-found confidence and freedom all he wanted to do was serve the King; His desire would be the prophet's service and delight.*

*So orders were given and the prophet was commissioned to go to the people on Earth, carrying a holy instruction."*

Divine encounter is one of the grand themes of Scripture. God interrupts both the godly and the ungodly, arrests them with the beauty and fear of His nature, and sets them on a different path. Paul, or Saul as he was called until he was encountered, was a one-man judge, jury and executioner. He was the inquisition against the group of people who called themselves, "The Way". What arrogance! How dare they say they are "the way"! But God had other plans. He interrupted the travels of this persecutor of Christ's followers and turned him into His advocate, representing the very people he had been persecuting! Now that is what I call a turn around.

Scripture is full of divine encounter. Noah becomes a type of Christ saving humanity … Abraham gets sent to a promised land … Moses is commissioned to rescue God's people … the Acts of the apostles is one long story of encounter after encounter and makes us aware of an acceleration of God appearing to mankind. Every hero of Scripture is a product of divine encounter. So when did we stop believing in divine encounter? Why has the Church rationalised encounter out of our thinking and gravitated towards programs, structures and traditions? The post-modern world we live in demands authenticity and needs an experience to validate its truths. That is why we need encounter! We need to regroup and focus on accessing the divine once again.

## Digging deeper

Church needs to stop being mediocre. Out of our desire for stability and routine we have sanctioned a "sameness" and safeness in church that makes it dull, devoid of any spark of life. And this is as true in the Spirit-filled stream of the Church as anywhere else. We are guilty of recalling our past, treasured experiences and trotting them out again in the hope that God will kiss them and make them live again. But we have our eyes on the wrong things, looking to the manifestations of God rather than to God Himself. We are more concerned about what God has done than finding the new "doings" of God. Pearl Hunters have to be people who are, frankly, a little bit unsatisfied about the way things are. I think Tim Hughes captures the pearl hunting zeal in his song, *Consuming Fire*:

*There must be more than this*
*O breath of God, come breath within*
*There must be more than this*
*Spirit of God we wait for You*
*Fill us anew we pray*
*Fill us anew we pray*

*Come like a rushing wind*
*Clothe us with power from on high*
*Now set the captives free*
*Leave us abandoned to Your praise*
*Lord let Your glory fall*
*Lord let Your glory fall*

*Consuming fire*
*Fan into flame*
*A passion for Your name*
*Spirit of God*
*Fall in this place*
*Lord have Your way*
*Lord have Your way*
*With us.*[161]

Our spirituality has got to be real, it has got to have life, it has got to work! We cannot be satisfied until we have found the pearl of great price, we cannot just sit back and trot out the old faithful songs, do the stuff that we have always done. There must be the *reality of encounter* in all that we give ourselves to. It is going to take a very determined church to not become a settling organisation, staying on the edge will take a hot coal flung from heaven and touching our lips; it will take a body of people determined to grab hold of their identity as the body of Jesus on earth and embrace its destiny in releasing the words of God to the world. Church, we have to dig in to God to get more of that which we seek!

## Rest and work

There is indeed work to be done as the Church, and we have to find a way of going beyond the froth and bubble of touchy-feely meetings, to get to the place of real power. It is going to take work and focus for us to see the fullness of the presence of God in our lives, in our communities. But not the "work" of human hands, no, a different sort of grit, a determination that bubbles up from the inner being, that emerges from people of character, that comes out of spiritual perseverance.

Working is part of the human makeup, part of our original design. There is nothing wrong with work, in fact it is intrinsic to our wellbeing. But frequently we allow "work" to replace the divine in our lives. Most of us live pressurised lives that are, to some extent, not of our making. As consumers we demand instant access and instant results; as producers we find it hard to keep up with the demand of our consumers. The more we producers produce, the more the consumer consumes. This vicious cycle speeds up over time and we strive to keep up until we get broken! That is modern living, unlike the hamster on the wheel we don't seem to know when to stop! Before we can learn about spiritual perseverance – a topic massively needed in a Church that wants to collapse on the sofa and give up – we first have to learn the art of *stopping*. The pressure we feel in just about every area of our lives is not the sort of life that God either created for us or wants for us. So before we can engage in the thrust of kingdom activity, we need to learn to adopt the rhythms of the divine.

## Adjusting our thinking!

*"Are you tired? Worn out? Burned out on religion? Come to me. Get away with me and you'll recover your life. I'll show you how to take a real rest. Walk with me and work with me—watch how I do it. Learn the unforced rhythms of grace. I won't lay anything heavy or ill-fitting on you. Keep company with me and you'll learn to live freely and lightly."* (Matthew 11:28 *The Message*)

One of the dilemmas I have to constantly grapple with, and I'm sure you are the same, is the balancing act between work and rest. If you are one of life's activists (like me), then the "doing" bit is easy and the "being" bit is okay for a day off! But to cultivate a life of just being? That is something altogether different. I have been in many meetings where the emphasis has been on being a "Mary", sitting at the feet of Jesus, rather than a "Martha", and my particular stream of churches has placed an emphasis on the need to "be" and not only "do". Many have followed this path because they are burned out on religion. The worst excesses of religious dogma have fried them to a crisp and many have been screwed up by a works-based spirituality.

Church, or shall we just call it religion, has a habit of burning us out and stopping us from getting any enjoyment from our faith in action. But while we focus on sitting at Jesus' feet and resting, we mustn't settle for a a theology of inactivity to cope with the devastating effects of overwork! Actually, Christ calls us to mission; He calls us to "go", so we must go! The important issue here is not the going (my last chapter will cover that) or the issue of works, but rather that we understand the need to seek spiritual rest and recuperation in order to be strengthened for the task ahead. Naturally speaking, our bodies need a good night's sleep in order to function well the next day. Our spiritual "inner man" is no different. We need to rest and recharge to function at our best. Life seems constantly to militate against us finding the stillness necessary for this to happen. There is little if any natural quietness any more. The "noise" of life conspires to keep our minds buzzing, so much so that stillness is almost alien to us. If we do find a "quiet moment" we are very likely to fill it with "sound" by turning on our iPod or the TV or picking up a magazine.

As a noisy Charismatic, I have always loved the vibrancy of loud worship, dancing, clapping and shouting. The thought of having a minute's silence, even on Remembrance Sunday, is foreign to our worship vocabulary. Anything involving noise is fine; anything involving silence seems a bit religious and to be avoided. Whilst all this has its place, we have certainly lost the value of silence. Yet occupying a place of stillness in God's presence is vital if we are to grow in Him. Jesus exemplified a way of living that embraced this proper balance.

## Learning to listen

Jesus was in full flow in His parable telling. He had just given His listeners the key kingdom parable, the one that would unlock His disciples' understanding (the parable of the sower [162]) when He launched into yet another parable. This time it was about hiding a lamp under a bowl[163], a parable about the revealing of the mysteries of the kingdom. We all know it is absurd to hide something like a light under a blanket. A light is supposed to be displayed to all! Jesus was telling us that the truths of the kingdom are like mysteries, they need to be revealed. This was one of Jesus' main jobs: to start revealing the mysteries of the kingdom. But I read in this parable not just an invitation to the unbeliever to grasp the mystery of the kingdom at a basic level. To me it is an invitation to go deeper into the things of God: *"... for all that is secret will eventually be brought into the open, and everything that is concealed will be brought to light and made known to all."* Remember, the context of these verses is Jesus opening up access to the kingdom of Heaven. He is not really talking about our personal secrets being exposed (although one day we will stand before our Maker), but about the mysteries and secrets of the kingdom. There is a treasure chest of mystery to be unveiled; there are pearls of wisdom and understanding currently locked up that are in the process of being revealed; they are available to us to go and access, because the way has been made open to us.

The passage in Luke goes on to say, *"pay attention to how you hear."* I am struck by this phrase, "how you hear". In the earlier passage on the sower, Jesus gives people very basic instruction on listening. He says simply, "Listen!" or in His words, "Anyone with ears to hear should listen and understand." Our greatest need is to just do some listening to God! How will we ever delve into the mysteries available for us to discover unless we tune into God? The great evangelistic challenge of our age, therefore, is to first get ourselves and then others to turn off the noise in their lives and listen to God for a moment. What is the alternative? The great Old Testament prophet puts it very starkly: *"... since they refused to listen when I called to them, I would not listen to them when they called to me!"*[164] Believers can be incredibly dull to the things of the Spirit because there is so much that can entice us away and numb our spiritual senses. We want the presence of God, yet we mask out that which could attune us to God! Instead we must learn to be like the young Samuel, who had to discern the voice of God speaking to him and eventually said, "Speak Lord, I am listening."[165]

## Deep listening

The parallel passage to the light under a bowl story[166] says *"pay close attention to what you hear."* Why? Because not all voices are God's voice. In my own journey of listening to God I have had to discern His voice from the voice of my own desires or enemy voices. This takes some time and does not come easily, but it can be done. Brother Lawrence in his classic, *The Practice of the Presence of God*, talks about "keeping the soul's gaze on God, within which always all is done quietly, humbly, lovingly and without giving way to any disturbance or anxiety." In my own rather half-hearted pursuit of this particular pearl I have had to try and learn silence and focus in my meditation. Another monastic classic gives the sage advice: "If you want to enter, live, and work in this cloud of unknowing, you will need a cloud of forgetting between you and the things of earth."[167] It's true: to journey into silence and stillness you need to switch off the sounds that bombard you; you have to surrender your own situation with all its pressures into God's hands. The temptation to pray for yourself, your needs, and others and their needs, and wander off into thinking about all the things you need to do is huge. Don't underestimate how much noise is in your head. Just try stopping for a short while and you will find out just how much sound is banging around inside! My introduction to silence in prayer was an enforced one by God. I found that for a whole year I was unable to pray anything much; all I felt compelled to do was sit in silence with God, learning how to listen!

"Pay attention to how you hear"[168] the scripture says. How do we hear? We can listen at one level, but there are so may aspects of the mystery of God that need to be uncovered. "Deep listening" is part of the tool bag of the Pearl Hunter. If you have ever met a deer hunter, you will have noted that they can pick up the scent of the animal easily. They know where the deer hang out, they know how they move, they know when they will scatter. In fact, a good hunter is listening and watching all the time to understand what the object of the hunt is going to do next. Similarly, seeking God is not about just turning up to worship services on a Sunday or going to as many conferences as we can; it is cultivating a lifestyle that constantly pursues God. The mature in faith go past the point of the basic principles of Christian living, although it is easy to lose the basics if we allow stuff to get in the way; the Pearl Hunter is a deep listener, they are seeking out the secret things of God, delving into His heart, prepared to pursue whatever He is doing. Pearl Hunters will jump on the next plane to visit the next revival outpouring (if that is what God tells them to do); they are going to sit in silence for hours; they are going to study; they are going to do whatever it takes to get the next hidden mystery. Like an Easter day egg hunt, we are going to search all round the garden of our lives to find the prize.

I don't buy the idea that accessing the pearl of the presence is reserved for the full-time ministering Christian elite! It is a priestly function, so if you are believer that includes you! I spent 15 years in business and believe that this time was precious in establishing many aspects of my faith. In that time I was a Pearl Hunter. Despite the noisy surroundings of generating money, dealing with staff, making decisions, pushing out into new ventures, I was dedicated in my spirit to discovering God. Just because my employment is now taken care of by the church, it doesn't mean that the noise is any different. In fact I am still concerned with generating money, dealing with staff, making decisions and pushing out into new ventures! The noise is the same, though the context is different. And I have not met a Christian minister or pastor who does not struggle with maintaining their prayer life and intimacy with God. It is a struggle common to all of us who are on the quest for a deeper life with God.

## Retreat

Deep listening requires us to take determined action. It requires effort. The first thing we have to do is rest. Without making space for rest we are going to get nowhere. Rest is critical to cultivating a deeper relationship with God. We are designed to need rest at regular intervals, which is why the Mosaic Law put a "day off" in place called the Sabbath. In the work of the ministry I have recognised the need to retreat from life in order to rest appropriately, because one of the issues with "full time Christian work" is that it is full time! Therefore I have to pull away regularly to find rest and have found that "retreat" is the best method for me. It has been commented on by a number of people that I am at my best when I have had a retreat! The following is a brief outline of how I approach it:

Retreats can scare the pants off people, but they are a valid and effective way of tuning out the noise and tuning into God. "What will I do for 2 or 3 days?" we wonder. In the run up to a retreat (normally three days before) I start to think about the stuff that I need to lay out to God. I have taken to writing these things down. Then, when the time arrives, I arrange a place where I can be alone. For me, a retreat is a solitary thing, since I spend most of my life with people. Although I am an extrovert by nature, I also recognise that for God to do business with me effectively, I must be alone. I am fortunate to have some wonderful friends who let me stay in their holiday cottage near the sea, or I will find one of the many retreat houses that are around. I don't suggest a commercial hotel, since they are designed to fill you with noise, not give you the space to retreat from distraction.

On one such retreat, I visited a place without TV or Internet and gosh, it was painful! It is not until you are alone for three days with no distractions that you realise how dependent you are on the noise of your life! Just before I go on retreat I gather

together any books that I want to read and the study Bibles I
may need. This is a bit of a comfort blanket to me, because I
don't like the thought of not having something to read and
because pursuing God through the writings of others is also
part of my Pearl Hunter's psyche. A retreat is a Pearl Hunter's
trip, so I intend to hunt in a variety of ways. The purpose of
my retreat is to equip me to be a better hunter, though it is
primarily about the hunt itself – I am seeking my God. So with
a mini-library in the back of the car I head off to my retreat
space on day one. The rest of day one is spent stilling myself
from the noise of life. I will sit and write down any further
issues that I need to deal with on post-it notes as they come to
mind. This is my method of de-cluttering my head of stuff. I
spend some time "soaking", basically lying on the floor (made
very comfortable by cushions – retreats don't have to be austere
you know!) listening to some great worship music. By filling
my head with inspirational stuff, I begin to push out the rubbish.
I allow the Holy Spirit to convict me of any sin that I have left
un-confessed to Him so that nothing will hinder the hunt.
Day one is all about getting still.

Days 2/3 of the retreat contain the meat for me. I will have a
plan for study, but more often than not the Lord will take me
to a passage of Scripture and I will dive off looking for pearls. I
allow the Spirit to guide me down passages and, as I go, I find
stuff. This is interspersed with maybe a walk, a drive to an old
abbey, eating of course, and praying as I go. At some point I
will take out my post-its and pray earnestly for every issue,
allowing the Spirit to guide me, but I give God all the issues.
Normally, on the final day of the retreat I will stop and just
wait. By this point it is much easier just wait on God in silence
and listen. A stream of ideas will often come at this point and I
tend to write them down as they come, journaling everything.
God reveals His heart for me, reveals His nature, reveals His

plans and it is exciting. I try to get packed up so I can get home for tea time with the family. I realise that at the end I need to re-engage with normal life. Retreat requires us to unwind and rewind, or otherwise those whom we love get the brunt end of some odd behaviour.

If you are a Peal Hunter you need get hunting. This is an inner search as much as it is about extending the kingdom. To hunt the presence is to delve into your inners, to search your spirit, to find God. If you are a business man, why not make a retreat a part of your routine. You would go to a conference, so why not a retreat? Teachers, why not take time out to seek God in half term? Have a few days to relax then pack your bags and retreat with God. It matters very little what you do, if you are a Pearl Hunter then it is the fact that you are seeking that is important. Make it a priority. Some go off to conferences to retreat, and that is fine. But for me, they are too full of people and noise to really seek God. There is no right answer for a retreat, I simply share my routine. Be creative, be diverse, be different if that works.

## The hunt is on!

At the start of this chapter I retold the story of Isaiah getting his commission from God. Perhaps he was on a special retreat to seek God's face when he got this revelation? But it was an astounding moment of God revealing Himself to His prophet. Isaiah came face to face with his humanity in this moment and he thought himself doomed. He was confronted by the ugliness of his sinful state against the brilliance of the holiness of the divine. But in a moment, his guilt was removed, a mere coal from the holy fire of God could wipe away his sin and equip him for the work of God, to be God's mouthpiece on earth. Wow! What a moment. It totally transformed Isaiah.

John, who was exiled to the island of Patmos, had a similar encounter with God. He was worshipping God when the Lord started to speak to him. He had face to face contact with Jesus, in which the Lord commanded him to write a book to various churches. John too felt as if he would die, but the reassurance of Jesus enabled him to write down everything that he was shown. After dictating seven letters to the angels of the churches, you would think that was enough. After that experience I would have been pretty rocked to my core. But John looks up and sees a door in Heaven and an invitation to "come up here"[169], to join in the heavenly activity, to get a better view of what is going on in Heaven!

That invitation still reverberates through history to everyone who will take God up on the offer. The invite is, "Will you go higher, deeper, further?" As a Pear Hunter my spirit fills with excitement at such an offer. Sure, it's scary, sure it's unknown, sure it will cost, but what an invitation! The call to go deeper in God is the call to faithfulness, holiness; it is the call to live the life that God intends us to live. It will require you to give up stuff, your own agenda, your own issues, in fact your life. But when the Pearl Hunter gets gripped by the pearl of great price, nothing will stop them from attaining it. They will take the offer that God has given and embrace it with everything they have.

Will you, "Come up here"?

## Endnotes

161. Copyright © 2002 Thankyou Music (admin. by EMI Christian Music Publishing). All rights reserved.
162. Luke 8:4-15, repeated in Matthew 13:1-23; Mark 4:1-25
163. Luke 8:15-19
164. Zechariah 7:13
165. 1 Samuel 3
166. Mark 4:24
167. The Cloud of Unknowing, ed. Bernard Bangley, Paraclete Press, p13
168. Luke 8:18
169. Revelation 4

CHAPTER

# Pearly Gates

**12**

Moses persuaded God to hold back His wrath from His people and set about constructing a safe place for the presence of God to dwell. The result was: God got to be with His people and the people were spared a full frontal blast of glory which would have toasted them! The dwelling of God in the Tabernacle was God's temporary plan. It would have been an amazing sight, watching the glory of God descend into the tent, so intense that even Moses, who was given incredible access to the presence of God, could not enter when God descended. God really decided to enter that earthly construction with His full self. It seems as if His entire presence was contained within the feeble structure![170]

## Hunting on the inside!

The full import of these verses should have a pretty life-changing affect on us, since God now chooses to dwell in our bodies by His Holy Spirit. We have become tabernacles of God, His incredible glory dwelling in us as individuals. Pentecost was a pretty big deal, signalling the descent of the Supreme Being into the fragile shells of humanity. I must admit to feeling completely inadequate to being a carrier of God inside me, if I'm honest. A lot of the time I forget that the very notion of carrying God is more than a theological construct or an intellectual understanding. But if I start to be defined by this theology that I carry the presence, I start to change. That's why true transformation begins with the renewal of the mind.[171] We have to accept the theology of Spirit-infilling not just as an idea, but as a reality.

As a Pearl Hunter, my job is to dig out the truth of the presence of God, the reality of the treasure, the depths of spiritual understanding. Pearl Hunters are not content with the last experience, or the last spiritual thrill, they are maniacs, extremists, radicals. I am not content to just accept my baptism in the Spirit as a one off experience, or talk glibly about being filled with the Holy Spirit as some sort of once in a lifetime experience. I want to grapple with the resting place of God, I want to dig down to understand with my spirit the reality of what lives inside me every day. How can the Holy Spirit dwell in me even even though I continue to sin? Even though I can be miserable and grumpy? That is the Pearl Hunter's quest, to be *"ever filled and stimulated with the Holy Spirit"* as Paul commanded.[172] It demands a continual determination to allow the full reign of the Holy Spirit within us.

It's funny to think that actually the pearl of inestimable value is right on the inside of us. The search is on within the deepest parts of our spirits for the Spirit that brings us life! We can see this in the searching of all the people who have gone before us. It is why the pursuit of the presence of God can so easily become an "in-house" pursuit or, if we are not careful, self-indulgent and navel gazing. It is easily done; we can lose our external reference points when we become consumed by pursuit. Like the moments when we lose all track of time, becoming consumed with the task at hand, so that external stimulus becomes a distraction from the goal of our endeavours. Some Charismatics have got bruised by being Pearl Hunters.

In times of great outpouring of the Spirit, we can sometimes become self-consumed because we are finding something of great value. To me it is more about understanding the hunting season: there are times when we must pursue and seek with a greater burning intensity that at other seasons.

I am not the sort of guy that goes out hunting to kill animals, not that I have a problem with it. But most hunters will tell you that there are seasons in which to hunt and seasons not to hunt. I wonder if pearl hunting for the presence is much the same? I have not managed, probably because of my fragility, to maintain a spiritual fervour that is without ceasing. Our modern pace doesn't seem to afford us the luxury of seasons: times of fallow where we can take time out to reflect or consider, as well as times to go on the chase. But pace and seasonality are essential if we are to endure for the long run. I have noticed that spiritually zealous people have a habit of burning out. We get excited about a move of God, only to be disappointed when the promised revival doesn't turn out to be what we expected! I think it is not the zeal that is wrong, oh God give me one zealous person for a hundred lukewarm-lethargic types! It is our lack of understanding of the seasonality of God that is wrong. We are not dealing with a tame God, this is a God of creativity and diversity; not a magnolia God, but the creator of marigold and magenta. Humanity has a need to be in control, to understand the totality of God, to get God back in His box. But God only puts Himself in a box to achieve a bigger purpose. And even when He puts Himself in the box (ark), He breaks out on regular occasions! Stop trying to define God. Stop expecting God to do the expected. Stop treating Him like an amusement arcade slot machine. God is God and will continue to operate as God! There is a season to go pearl hunting and a season to go quiet and prepare for the pearl hunt. Sometimes we are so ill-equipped to be Pearl Hunters; we have faulty equipment, wrong expectations, incorrect intelligence. If only we would stop and sort out our stuff, then the pearl hunt would be so much more exhilarating!

## Hunting together

Once you have started to dig into the depths of the deposit of the Spirit on the inside of you, there is an even more powerful manifestation of the presence of God to pursue. He is resident in *US*. The Church is the depositary of the collective nature of the Spirit of God. In other words, He seeks to dwell in us, together! I suppose that is why I remain an optimist for the Church. I see a glorious Church, shining and resplendent. It is why Isaiah starts to wax lyrical about the mountain of the Lord's house being predominant among others.[173] It grieves me to my core when I hear of believers who have all but given up with church. Perhaps church has bruised them, or not delivered on its promise, or abused them in some way? Perhaps they are completely justified out of self-defence to put up a boundary around their lives and say that the church will not hurt them anymore? If you can see yourself in that description, can I urge and appeal to you not give up, to try again, to forgive and keep forgiving as many times as you need to? We are supposed to hunt for the glory of God, the abiding presence, together. We are being beautified into the collective Bride of Christ. There is only one Bride for the Bridegroom, despite our best endeavours to make the returning Christ a bigamist by our endless schism and division of petty detail. Just one Bride, and that includes those who have de-churched themselves.

We really don't get to see the return of Christ until there is an unstoppable movement of believers operating as one in the kingdom task of the transformation of society. With my bony finger outstretched towards you like Lord Kitchener, I say "His kingdom needs you!" Church is not an optional extra for the believer, it is scratched into the very essence of belief. Belief can not be achieved in the absence of community. Sure, you can try, but ultimately a private belief system is a virus that stops fruitfulness; it is like choosing barrenness over fertility. I think the prophetic cry that we need to hear is the call for harvesters and Pearl Hunters to galvanize in the search for true riches. We find the treasure of the presence of God in ourselves and we find it in each other. I don't have a private monopoly on the fullness of the expression of God, part of my treasure is found in my brother and my sister, and they may not even be saved yet! Evangelism isn't just about plucking the wretched sinner from eternal damnation, it is about finding the treasure of the presence of God in each other, deciding to see the goodness of God in another person. They may be angry, abusive, judgmental, bigoted, deviant – but yet in each one of us there is a deposit of something of the divine, and in each one of us there is the opportunity to shine! I think some of the heroes of the faith who sit in the mud and dirt with the poorest of our global society, must do so because they catch a glimpse of the divine treasure in everyone. You couldn't do it, could you, unless you believed in the deposit of godliness on the inside? We are supposed to hunt together for the pearl of great price precisely because that pearl is in each of us.

We must belong together in a local church, however that is expressed. It matters very little to God whether it is denomina-tional, organic, simple, big, loud, solemn, or whether we read our prayers from a script or roar like lions. If the Spirit of God is there, it is God's Church. Local churches must belong to something, together. Theologically, independence doesn't make any sense at all. Scripture encourages inter-dependence, where we are woven together and connected. Whether that is a network, a partnership, a link or a denomination, the Church of Jesus Christ is a connected life-form. Like the Asherah poles of the

Old Testament, we must pull down the strong idolatry of "independence". It is not for me, however, to force you to pull down your independence, it is for you to be softened by the Spirit and for you to tear down the barriers of independence yourself.

## Have we stopped hunting?

I'm going to be a little bolder now that you have reached the end of the book and the chances of you not reading the last few pages are pretty slim! Western Christianity has got itself into a mess. We have forgotten what we are about. We have replaced our first love with a programme. We have become slick to appeal to the masses. We try to be like the world we are trying to save. We have settled, rather than continuing to pioneer. We have forgotten the stories of God's deliverance and favour, and embraced rationalism, excusing our lack of power and sidelining the reality of the Spirit. Many of us have become fed up with church not working and so have settled for the status quo rather than pressing in for the promise. It's a mess! We hunger for power, yet have made a pact with cultural values alien to holiness, but as long as we compromise spiritually then the heavenly power we seek will elude our grasp. We long for the manifestation of the authentic glory of God, yet we explain away ethical and moral priorities as not being socially relevant. We act like we love our neighbours, yet have forgotten the love paradigm that should pervade our souls. We call pride "excellence" and greed "blessing". Dearly beloved of God, it is time to get our house in order and sort out the mess that it has fallen into!

Haggai the prophet delivered a stinging attack on the Zerubbabel, Governor of Judah, and Joshua the High Priest. They were effectively sitting on their hands, doing nothing, while Solomon's glorious temple lay in ruins after the sacking of Jerusalem. Cyrus, the ruler of the region at the time, had declared that the people of God could return to Jerusalem after being exiled for 70 years. So the first batch of immigrants returned to Jerusalem and in their enthusiasm rebuilt the altar of the Lord on the desolate place of the old temple. But the people of God had been away for so long that a new "pagan" set of inhabitants had made Jerusalem their home, and they were pretty hacked off with the pompous returning Hebrews. The new residents complained so much that work on the temple stopped and a new status quo was developed for the next 20 years – i.e. nothing happened. The Governor, Zerubbabel, was just keeping the peace and pleasing the people. The great project to rebuild the temple ground to a halt.

Well, God is pretty patient, so He raises up a prophet called Haggai and delivers a between-the-eyeballs prophetic word to the Governor, the High Priest and, indeed the people: "Look," says God through Haggai, "the people may be saying that the season is not right to rebuild My Temple, but this is not a democracy. I AM telling you it is time to get on with it. You have refurbished your homes, you have started to get rich, you have got your businesses working, but My House is still a pile of rubble! I think you have got your priorities all wrong. You have all got too comfortable in your lukewarm lifestyles, you have settled and forgotten what you had returned to do. Actually you are not being at all productive, you are not getting much of a return for your efforts, you are not really being satisfied by your endeavours, your wages just disappear like water. Get on with building My House. Make the main thing the main thing. Put your efforts into the place of my Presence, then perhaps the harvest that you desire will happen".[174]

This word from God put the wind up Zerubbabel and Joshua (I can't imagine what the High Priest was doing for 20 years with no temple to run. Perhaps he was in meetings?!) and they repented and galvanized the whole Hebrew community to get on with the job of restoring the temple. I think that this Haggai prophecy is for us today. This is what the Church needs to hear and become focused on doing. There has been a gross neglect of the House of the Lord, both as the temple of our bodies and collectively as the Church. We have allowed the voices of paganism, disguised as theology, and sociology to infiltrate the community of God's people. We have somehow got lost on the journey, forgotten what we are doing here, taken a wrong turn and settled. We probably started the rebuilding program at one time or another, but we have largely forgotten what it was all about. We had lots of good intentions to rebuild the temple, we meant to focus on it, but somehow these have been lost to our jobs, our families, our social pursuits, our self interest, our comfort! If you are a church leader, perhaps conferences have become a distraction? Perhaps programmes have taken over what started as a Spirit thing? Perhaps all you are doing now is remembering the good old days, rather than living in the New Day?

If there one thing I want to provoke you to do, it is to reorder your priorities and become a Pearl Hunter once again. Stop looking for answers anywhere else and get looking for the awesome presence of God. Get out of the comfort zone of your sedate life, decide to press in, renew your enthusiasm for the chase. If we make the presence of God the main thing, then blessing will follow, people will get saved, and personal fulfilment will happen. But we need to be presence seekers and to put the priorities of God's House ahead of our own personal interests. The debate about our priority being either the worship of God or the saving of souls is frankly pathetic. One flows from the other. To hear evangelists say that we can worship God in Heaven, but we can only save people here on earth, so our priority must be evangelism is unbiblical nonsense. We are supposed to love God and love others. These are two sides of the same coin. In fact, I think there is a cap on our ability to lavishly love God until we have done some loving of others!

## Keep hunting

Modern believers have lost some of the grit of determination that I read about in the stories of the saints of the past. Even when you sit with an older believer, you get the distinct impression that modern Christians have it easy and are frankly wimps compared to the generations that have gone before them. We pretty much cop out of stuff far too soon. We don't tend to stick at it. We allow ourselves off the hook far too easily. Scripture, however, is full of injunctions to keep going, to not give up, to stand firm, to persevere and endure to the end. Why? Because the writers know how tough it can be. We must not embrace the spirit of our age that cries out for personal comfort, individualism and freedom of choice. Don't misread what I am saying, hear the Spirit. Our comfort can be a blessing, individualism admired and freedom is good. But our pursuit of the presence is more important than all of these things and we may have to sacrifice them. When we seek first the kingdom everything else we need for life will follow on![175]

## On the move

The human inclination to settle is part of the problem we face. When we stop pioneering and start to inhabit, a lethargy comes over us. Instead we need to keep our pioneering spirit while taking the territory God mandates us to take. I have lived in the same town for 24 years, yet I still feel like a pioneer. The story of the people of God is a story of journey and movement. When they settled too long and started to mate with the local girls the rot started to set in. Movement is key!

Personally, I like change, but I have come to see that most people don't like it. In fact, it has taken me many years to understand that there are people who like things to stay exactly as they are, and this is how they feel safe. I'm just not convinced that God works like that. There is something in the heart of a Pearl Hunter that has to be a change junkie. Believers have to love risk, love adventure, love to try new things. I don't have any great advice for you if that seems a bit frightening. The urge to keep everything the same is alien to me. The kingdom mandate is to subdue the Earth and everything in it. We are supposed to conquer our territory and that means doing new things and keeping on the move. Everything we do should have the stamp of the Pearl Hunter on it. We are pushing the boundaries of the Kingdom to make space for the rule of God. The glory of the presence of God is supposed to fill the earth[176], through you and me. The mandate of the Kingdom of God is to release the presence of God in everything we do and everything we say.

Friends, we are a people on the move. At the end of the exodus story, the glory falls and fills the tabernacle so that Moses cannot stand up.[177] But when it was time to go on the next leg of the journey, the glory of the Lord would lift, the people of God would pack up the tent and move on to the next location, following the cloud or fire. That's church, or at least it is supposed to be. We must be hanging on every movement of God! May God send the Church prophets to tell us what He is doing and where He is going if we can't figure it out for ourselves! I do not want to be left behind in an empty tabernacle when God has long since moved on. Many of us are lagging behind: we worship Sunday by Sunday in a building that is a testimony to a previous move of God, but the Holy Spirit moved on ages ago. Can I suggest that you pack up and find out where the Holy Spirit is now? If necessary, lock up your building, seek Him out, and when you find Him, then decide what to do with the facility you've built for Him. God will occupy that space with presence and power if only you will invite Him!

Movement is part of our missional mandate. As we follow the presence of God we cannot help but be missional. Of course we need to see people saved; of course we are rescuers; of course we are to infiltrate society with the message of love and redemption. But we are to do so from the place of the presence of God. If we prioritise the presence, we will be filled with His glory and then have something to go and tell people about. Too often our evangelism has been done out of duty. We are following the Great Commission; we know we "ought to" do it, although we hate the idea of talking to someone about Jesus! When we are presence people, however, the "ought to" becomes the excited story of a child. When my little girl gets excited about something, she can't wait to tell me all about it. She bubbles over with excitement about her day or her latest project. When we are having fun, when we are fulfilled, when we are in love, try and stop us telling other people! Contagious evangelism is the product of presence-filled lives, not programme-driven learning.

## Converging realities

When the presence of God goes with us we should live authentic lives, we should hear His voice, we should experience heavenly encounters, and we should believe that we have divine power. When we start a journey of experiencing God, we start to believe different things about Him. We experience the love of a Father, so are able to love those around us. We experience the rights of sons of God, so are able to rise above our circumstances. We experience His healing in our emotions and bodies, so are able to start to give it away. The experience of the divine is essential if we are to live our physical lives in the way they were always intended to be lived. God created our physical bodies to contain His Spirit; we are supposed to be a convergence of physical and spiritual realities. The exciting thing is that as these realities come closer together, the potential to release the Kingdom becomes ever more apparent. This is why we see a dramatic change in the disciples after the Holy Spirit fills them. Suddenly, the reality of Jesus' teaching makes sense. All this Kingdom stuff becomes real because the Holy Spirit fills the training that Jesus has given them. The convergence of realities: our lives suddenly makes sense when the presence of God collides with our humanity. Now we have the power to live out the reality of God's Kingdom and take territory.

## Territory taker

Joshua really got this idea. Joshua, Moses' intern and deputy, eventually becomes the leader of the movement. He is full of faith, learns to see things right and understands the presence of God. So when the moment comes for the old man to pass on the baton, he gives it to the obvious candidate, his spiritual son, Joshua. Joshua understood the idea of territory taking, motivated by the presence, propelled by the voice of God and empowered with heavenly fuel. Nothing could stop Joshua. As soon as the words ring out that "Moses is dead," God speaks to him promising the fullness of the promise he gave Moses: *"Wherever you set foot, you will be on the land I have given you."*[178] It's a pretty amazing promise! It sounds like God trusts this dude if he is willing to back him up like that. God mandates Joshua to do great things, but he has to be a presence man. He has to understand that he needs to dwell on the words God has spoken all the time if he is to be successful. In short, if Joshua doesn't stick close to his God, then he's stuffed!

The people had learnt their lesson too. They basically said to Joshua, whatever you tell us to do, we will do. They got the message that obedience was being aligned to the presence of God. They were not going to mess up like their ancestors did in the past. They were not going to screw it up again. No, this time they would say, "Yes sir … how high sir?" This time, when the spies searched the land, they gave a faith-filled report rather than scaremongering. As they moved out behind the presence of God-in-a-box, Joshua accessed divine power and the seas parted. This guy had got it; he knew how to move in the authority of God; he knew how to harness spiritual authority to move earthly forces.

Joshua is an incredible template of kingdom territory taking. We are supposed to carry on this work of taking territory. We may not be an invading army occupying land and subduing people groups, but we are an invading army waging war against spiritual dominions that have taken up residence in the land. Legally, we want to get our land back. The spiritual squatters have become long term tenants and now they are pretending that they own the land. We, the Church, have turned our backs for a moment and the dark spiritual forces have taken territory that belongs to us. In the UK, the Church crusaded for better housing and health care and eventually our Government did something about it. But the Church turns its back for a decade or two and now finds it hard to get into our social welfare and healthcare systems. The scientific-rationalist-secularist agenda has squeezed us out, only allowing a faint respect for established religion that won't challenge the now strong power base of the spiritual forces.

If the Church is ever to regain its Kingdom territory taking again, it must be through a presence-filled community, a people who are in touch with their heavenly identity, and who as sons of Heaven can take the power that is theirs into the Earth.

## Nearing the gates

This Pearl Hunter is about to sign off. But like Abraham who saw a city whose architect was God[179] I have tried to communicate something of what I see in my spirit, even if my faltering vocabulary doesn't do justice to the amazing vision of what is in store for the people of God. I think this is why the book of Revelation is so gripping, because John gets to share the real picture of Heaven using the imagery of earth to communicate the majesty of the spiritual dwelling place. I think I need to borrow his imagery to close out this book.

Loosely paraphrasing Revelation 21:9-27:

"As we journey towards the destination of our souls, this shining city descends from on high, something coming down to us. It is like one huge precious stone, a diamond sparkling and glowing. The walls of this city are high and thick, entrances clearly marked and guarded by angelic sentries. Seeing the walls closer, they are jasper red and crystal like in quality. The walls are not built on rubble, but sapphires, agates, beryl, topaz and all manner of beauty. I stand in front of a gate, and finally I see what all this hunting has been about. The gate is not made from wood or steel, no, I stand at the gate, the very object of my desire and it is fashioned from one single pearl. Surely I have found the final object of my pursuit, the ultimate prize. Walking through the permanently open gates a golden hue hits me. There is no temple here, no separation from God's presence, no need for a sun or a moon, because the radiant presence of God fills the whole place. Now all the nations can bring their praise and glory to the Lord of all. Now those who are on the list get full and free access, nothing hindering the flow of the people of God from their King."

This city coming down must be our object. We take dominion on this earth to prepare the territory for the arrival of the City of God. Not a city "up there somewhere", no, a city that will come to Earth. The story of the merchant pursuing the pearl of great price finds its ultimate prize in this city. The pearl, the very gateway to God, is the entrance to His Presence. For me, this heavenly scene stirs my quest. I want to spend my life pursuing that which is of great value and disposing of that which has no value at all. I want to spend my days hunting out the gates of pearl, bringing the Presence of God on earth for all to see. It is not worth crowding our lives out with things that have no eternal value. Instead we are made to be daily pursuers of the City of Presence. Now that is worth the hunt!

## Endnotes

170. Exodus 40:34-38
171. Romans 12:2
172. Ephesians 5:18, Amplified Bible
173. Isaiah 2:2
174. Haggai 1
175. Matthew 6:33
176. Numbers 14:21
177. Exodus 40
178. Joshua 1:3
179. Hebrews 11:10